THE JEWISH HERITAGE SERIES

GOD AND THE STORY OF JUDAISM

THE JEWISH HERITAGE SERIES

GOD AND THE STORY OF JUDAISM

DOROTHY K. KRIPKE *teacher and writer*
MEYER LEVIN *novelist and playwright*
TOBY K. KURZBAND *principal, New York City Public Schools   general editor*

STEPHEN KRAFT *art editor*

LORENCE F. BJORKLUND *illustrations*

BEHRMAN HOUSE, INC. PUBLISHERS   NEW YORK, N.Y.

Copyright 1962 by Behrman House, Inc., 1261 Broadway, New York 1, N. Y.
Manufactured in the United States of America
Library of Congress Catalog Card Number: 62-17078

Foreword to the Teacher

With the publication of GOD AND THE STORY OF JUDAISM by Dorothy K. Kripke and Meyer Levin, THE JEWISH HERITAGE SERIES acquires both a new beginning and a fulfillment. Although it is the third volume in the order of appearance, it is first in the primacy of its concepts and will now precede the other two in the order of teaching.

THE JEWISH HERITAGE SERIES was originally introduced with the assumption that Jewish religious education can be most meaningful to our children if it relates to their own immediate experience and if it answers questions in which Jewish concepts and values are brought to bear on these experiences.

We began with THE STORY OF THE SYNAGOGUE because the course out of which the book had developed was one of the first to put this point of view into practice. The synagogue (and its school) was the most tangible contact our pupils could have with organized Jewish life outside the home. Beginning with the ceremonial objects and observances which pupils could experience directly, they were led back into the origins of Jewish worship and introduced to the many and varied forms this worship has assumed throughout Jewish history.

The second volume, THE STORY OF THE JEWISH WAY OF LIFE, extended this idea into the larger Jewish community. Beginning with the Jewish "ways of life" which children could observe in their own community, it also went back into the Jewish past to discover the origins of this way of life and how it changed throughout history—with particular emphasis on the Eastern European Jewish community of the 17th century, the effects of the Emancipation in Western Europe and America, and the old-new way of Jewish life developing in Israel.

In determining the nature of the third volume in this series, we faced a problem that has been of the most vital concern to Jewish religious educators in recent years. With the growing interest in Jewish religious ideas, every one now agrees that our pupils should have a clear and meaningful understanding of Jewish teachings about God. The question has largely been one of method. One point of view has been that the Jewish concept of God should permeate every course and should be both implicit and explicit, as pupils learn about the festivals, the observances and the institutions of Jewish life and the study of Jewish history and literature and the Hebrew language. This was the approach taken in the first two volumes of THE JEWISH HERITAGE SERIES.

In the most recent deliberations of Jewish religious educators there has been a growing agreement that this "indirect" teaching of the Jewish ideas about God should be supplemented by a "direct" teaching of these ideas and that this must be done as early as possible in the curriculum. One of the pioneers representing this point of view has been Dorothy K. Kripke. In her first volume, "Let's Talk About God," published by Behrman House in 1953, parents and teachers found a book which answered children's first questions about God in clear and vivid language and with a point of view that skillfully combined traditional concepts and modern interpretations. In her succeeding volumes, "Let's Talk About Right and Wrong" and "Let's Talk About Judaism," Mrs. Kripke extended these ideas to the ethics and practices of Judaism on a primary level.

In this volume, GOD AND THE STORY OF JUDAISM, Mrs. Kripke has joined with Meyer Levin, co-author of THE STORY OF THE SYNAGOGUE and THE STORY OF THE JEWISH WAY OF LIFE, to create a new and significant textbook for the intermediate grades to introduce THE JEWISH HERITAGE SERIES in the curriculum.

Once again, Meyer Levin has brought to this partnership the talents of a creative writer combined with a deep religious feeling steeped in Jewish traditions. The knowledge and attitudes which pupils will acquire as a result of reading this book will make the succeeding years' studies even more meaningful and significant.

In the previous volumes, there were two types of questions at the end of each chapter. One was for *pupils* to think about, and the other was to share with their *parents*. In this volume these two types of questions are again used. Because of the nature of the subject, it is particularly important that teachers use all their skills to motivate the questions which the children will be asked to bring home to their parents. It is equally important that parents also read this book to know what will be ahead of them and to prepare themselves by additional reading and study so that their children will receive the benefit of their parents' knowledge and convictions. An *Activity Book* suggesting classroom procedures and elaborating home assignments is also available.

TOBY K. KURZBAND

Contents

UNIT ONE

How Judaism Began

CHAPTER	I	Long Ago People Believed in Many Gods	12
CHAPTER	II	How Abraham Understood There Was One God	17

UNIT TWO

What Judaism Teaches Us About God

CHAPTER	III	We Cannot See God But We See His Work	24
CHAPTER	IV	God Created the World and All Things in It	29
CHAPTER	V	God Made Order in the World	35
CHAPTER	VI	God Created Man	41
CHAPTER	VII	God Gave Man Special Gifts	46
CHAPTER	VIII	God in History	53
CHAPTER	IX	God Is Different From People	60
CHAPTER	X	We Cannot Know Everything About God	65

UNIT THREE

What Judaism Teaches Us About Right and Wrong

CHAPTER	XI	We Can Choose Between Right and Wrong	72
CHAPTER	XII	Why Should We Choose What Is Right?	77

UNIT FOUR — What Judaism Teaches Us About the Right Way

CHAPTER XIII	Justice Is the Right Way	84
CHAPTER XIV	Charity, Mercy and Love Are the Right Ways	91
CHAPTER XV	Brotherhood Is the Right Way	98
CHAPTER XVI	Self-Respect and Humility Are the Right Ways	103
CHAPTER XVII	Honesty Is the Right Way	109
CHAPTER XVIII	Repentance and Forgiveness Are the Right Ways	116
CHAPTER XIX	Hillel's Rule Is the Right Way	122

UNIT FIVE — What Judaism Teaches Us About Life

CHAPTER XX	The World We Live in Is Good	128
CHAPTER XXI	Life Is to Be Enjoyed	136
CHAPTER XXII	Trouble Is Part of Life	143

UNIT SIX — What Judaism Teaches Us About Prayer

CHAPTER XXIII	We Talk to God Through Prayer	150
CHAPTER XXIV	We Pray In a Synagogue	156
CHAPTER XXV	A Prayer Book Helps Us to Pray	164
CHAPTER XXVI	There Are Times to Pray	170
CHAPTER XXVII	There Are Many Kinds of Prayer	176
CHAPTER XXVIII	Study Is Part of Prayer	182

In memory of Max and Goldie Karp and Dr. Meyer Steinberg

UNIT ONE

How Judaism Began

CHAPTER I

Long Ago People Believed in Many Gods

When you first began to wonder about everything around you, you asked, "Who made the world? Who made the sky? Who made the stars? Who made lions and horses and crocodiles and goldfish? Who made me?"

And the answer was, "God."

And then, didn't you ask, "Who made God?"

And the answer was, "God."

God was the beginning.

Perhaps you thought that was not enough of an answer.

You asked, "What is God? What does He look like?"

And the answer was, "We cannot know what He looks like."

And perhaps you thought, "They don't know very much. They don't even know the main thing."

But when you were told we cannot know what He looks like you *were* told the main thing.

Everyone wonders about God

Long ago people imagined they knew what God looked like. Each tribe and each nation on earth imagined this in its own way. Some thought He looked like a man with a beard. Others thought He looked like a man with the head of an eagle. Still others thought He looked exactly like their own king.

Of course all of them were wrong. But all of them were right in their desire to know God. And still today we try to know about God, not about what He looks like, for we know that God is invisible, but we try to discover the *meaning* of God.

Your parents and your teachers and your rabbi and the wise men of the world have always sought this meaning. You too will search for it all of your life. But you can begin by learning what we have already discovered to be true and what we have already found out to be wrong.

The first thing people are likely to imagine about God is that God is like people. Children often imagine that God is like a wise old man with a long white beard. And in ancient times, grownups often had this same idea. For unless they study and think, grownups often keep the same ideas they started out with as children.

Long ago people made up stories about the gods

In olden times, people believed that a god was like a very wonderful person and that there were many gods. Often they believed there was a main god, like a father or a grandfather, and that he had a whole family of gods.

They believed that, just like people, gods were born, and that they married and had children. But they did not believe that gods died. They said that gods were immortal.

This was the first thought that came to them to help them discover what God was really like. For as you know, discoveries happen little by little. It sometimes takes centuries for a whole discovery to be made. And so it was with people's thoughts about God.

At first, people made up stories about their gods. They told stories about gods being hungry, and having special kinds of food and drink, like nectar and ambrosia. They believed that gods could quarrel and have wars. When there was thunder in the sky, they said the gods were fighting.

You can see how natural it is to imagine such a thing. Suppose you were born in olden times before scientists had discovered how lightning and thunder were made. When you heard the great rumbling of thunder in the sky, you could tell yourself a story about the chariots of great gods, rumbling across the skies in their battle.

You may still tell yourself such stories today. But you know they are

Long ago people believed lightning and thunder came from the gods

made-up stories, because you know there is a natural cause of thunder. But in the old days people did not know the natural causes, and so they believed their own stories.

They also believed their gods had jobs to do, and that each god had his special job. The god of hunting gave them meat to eat. The god of war had to help them win their battles, and if they lost they were angry with him.

The sun-god and the moon-god

Almost the first god that people made up was the god of the sun. For people everywhere saw the round fire-red sun shining in the sky. They felt its comfortable warmth. They were happy in its light. They saw that the growing plants of the earth turned to face the sun. And they saw that the touch of the sun's rays made the green things greener and the red apples redder.

People knew, without really understanding it, that there could be no life on earth without the heat and light of the sun. Therefore, many people decided the sun was god.

Then, in the night, they were afraid of the dark. When they saw the moon that made the dark night bright, they decided there was a god in the moon, too. And it was natural for them to think that since there were men and women in the world, there must be a man god and a woman god. So they imagined the sun was the man god and the moon was the woman god, or goddess.

King-gods and other gods

Sometimes people even believed a living person was a god. Their king, for instance. They knew he had the power to rule their lives. He had armies that marched at his command. They saw his palaces, his golden crown, and his jewels. And they bowed down and worshipped him as a god. Sometimes they made up a story that their king was born from a family of gods. Therefore, they said, their king was a god.

Still other people invented a god for each thing that they could not explain. They told themselves that each wonder in nature was controlled by its own god. There were river gods and there were gods of the mountains; there was a god of lightning; there was a god of the sea.

They also believed there were gods for special wishes. There was a god of love, a god of wisdom, a god of health, and a god of wealth.

And there were tribes who believed that not only each tribe but each family had its own special god. A family god might be in the form of a favorite animal or bird. Or it might be some magical stone that they imagined could protect them from harm. We can see examples of family gods on totem poles.

If the power of their god did not

Indian totem pole

work and they were conquered, then they were quite ready to change their gods and worship the gods of their conquerors. But still, they might secretly worship their old gods, too.

How people worshipped their gods

What was their worship? How did people go about worshipping all these gods that they had made up for themselves?

They needed to feel their gods were close to them, just as you sometimes want to feel there is a policeman right there where you can see him, ready to protect you. So they made statues and idols of their gods, that they could see and touch. They liked to have these images right inside the house.

And then they tried to please their gods or make bargains with them. They placed food and drink before their statues, the very best food they had. Sometimes they gave their gods the things they loved most. It was like a bribe to their gods to be good to them. They burned incense before their gods. They danced, and bowed down.

They also did some of the things that we do today; they had ceremonies, and they prayed. For the feeling in their hearts was a true wish to find God, and even if they imagined that God was inside a clay idol, those prayers that came from their hearts could be true prayers. But of course

15

true prayers do not need idols and are even more true without them.

Many bad things were done because people thought idols were real gods. They told themselves that anything they wanted to do could be helped by bribes or bargains with their gods. They imagined that whatever they wanted, their gods wanted. So if they wanted to kill their neighbors, they danced and made sacrifices to their gods and said their gods wanted it.

They did many dreadful things, such as sacrificing human beings to their idols.

And then, long ago, the truth about God came into the mind and heart of one man.

Who was this man? We will learn about him in the next chapter.

What we have learned so far

We have seen how people always needed to know about God. In every part of the earth, among the Africans, Greeks, and Chinese and Indians there are ancient stories about gods. For, long ago, people imagined there were many gods in the sky, or that there were magical gods in rocks and rivers, or that there were special gods for each tribe and family. They were just like children who make up stories and then believe their own stories. And they imagined they could bargain with their gods, by burning fine food before them, or making sacrifices. After they had all these childish ideas, how did people really learn about God?

QUESTIONS TO THINK ABOUT

1. In this chapter, you learned that the knowledge of God begins with wonder. Do you remember any questions you ever asked when you wondered about God?
2. What are some of the most important ways in which Jewish ideas about God are different from those of other peoples of long ago?

QUESTIONS TO ASK YOUR PARENTS

1. Some of these ideas about God which were believed by peoples of long ago are described in this chapter as "childish" ideas. Ask your parents if they can remember any "childish" ideas you had about God when you were a very young child.
2. Ask your parents what we substitute today for the sacrifices that our ancestors made long ago.

CHAPTER II

How Abraham Understood There Was One God

The first man to understand and proclaim that there was One God was Abraham. In the ancient city of Ur, filled with idol worshippers, Abraham declared there was One God, of heaven and earth.

You may think, "Why, anyone would know that!"

But if, like Abraham, you were born among people who believed in many idols, and if you were taught to worship them, how would you discover all by yourself that this was wrong?

We do not know how Abraham made his great discovery. We know only very little about his early days. The Bible tells us that he was the son of Terach and that they lived on "the other side of the great river" in the city of Ur. And this was more than 3,500 years ago.

Until our own times, no one could be sure that there ever was such a place as Ur, except for the Bible. But you know that in modern times many of the cities named in the Bible have been dug up, and Ur was one of those.

Archeologists have found this ancient city, and in their diggings they have found many such clay idols as were worshipped by the people of Ur in the time of Abraham.

The people of Ur worshipped idols of the sun and of the moon, gods of fertility and many other gods.

Stories tell us that Abraham was the son of a man who made such idols. But surely, even before the time of Terach and his son Abraham, there were other idol-makers who had sons. And none of those boys seems to have wondered whether the idols in his father's shop really and truly were gods.

Abraham smashes the idols

According to one of the legends told by the Rabbis, his father left him alone to tend shop one day, and a poor old woman came in, with a bowl of gruel.

She wanted to place the gruel as an offering before one of the idols. "As soon as I have money, I will buy the idol," she said. "But in the meantime, let me bring my offerings to it, here."

Abraham had recognized the little old woman. "But did you not buy a large idol from my father, only a short time ago?" he asked.

"Yes," she said, "but great misfortune has befallen me, and I need another idol to protect me. Thieves came and robbed my house," she told him. "They took everything I possessed. All I have left is a little gruel."

"But didn't the idol protect you?" the boy asked.

"They stole the idol too!" she wailed.

Then, even though he was sorry for her, Abraham couldn't help laughing. "If the idol itself was stolen," he asked, "how do you think another idol can protect you?" And he said to her, "Look, an idol has a mouth, but it cannot speak; it has eyes, but it cannot see; feet, but it cannot walk; ears, but it does not hear! How can you worship such a god that is helpless even before a simple thief?"

The old woman went away, leaving her bowl of gruel.

Abraham felt that it was all wrong. Suddenly he took a stick and began to smash the idols. He knocked them over, and one after another they broke into pieces. Only a single large idol was left unharmed, the one before

Abraham smashing the idols

which the old woman had placed her bowl of gruel. Instead of smashing it, Abraham placed the stick in its hands.

When Terach came home, he cried out, "What happened!"

"A battle of the gods!" said Abraham. "An old woman came and left this bowl of gruel for an offering. At once, a battle broke out among the idols. Each one cried out that the offering was for him! While they fought over it, the largest one picked up this stick—and you can see for yourself! He destroyed them all!"

Abraham's father was angry. "Don't tell me such stories!" he shouted. "An idol cannot speak! It cannot see! It cannot move its arms to strike!"

"If that is so," Abraham asked his father, "then how can the idols be gods?"

The truth about God

The story does not tell us whether Abraham was punished. For the story has something more important to tell us. This legend from the Rabbis tells us that this bright young boy saw the uselessness and foolishness of idol worship. He saw that *the idols were not really gods.*

That was the first great step. For when we know what is *not*, we can search for what *is*.

And Abraham searched for the truth about God.

How did he search? He must have wondered and wondered, just as we do still. He must have puzzled and dreamed, and waited for something inside himself to tell him.

And one day he must have had an inspiration.

And what is an inspiration?

An inspiration is a new understanding, a new vision that comes. We don't know from where. Poets have inspirations, when suddenly the words of a beautiful poem come into their minds. Inventors have inspirations when suddenly they see in their minds how a new machine will work. Prophets had inspirations when suddenly they felt they knew the ways of God.

And so one day an inspiration came to Abraham, and he knew that all he could see around him—the tiniest blade of grass under his hand, and the great sun so far away, and the people in the fields, and the birds—all creation was the work of God, One God. And he understood that God was so vast that man could never see Him in an image or an idol. God was invisible! And at the same time, Abraham understood that God was *everywhere*.

We can feel how Abraham must have felt at that moment. He must have felt filled with joy, filled with wonder. He must have felt, "This is the great truth! Everyone will understand it at once! I'll run and tell them!"

And so he began to tell people about God.

Abraham leaves Ur

But they didn't understand it at once. They had their idols, and they didn't want to hear about Abraham's God. And they simply could not understand about a God that was invisible, and that was everywhere all the time.

And so Abraham must not have been very popular.

In the town of Ur people must have spoken against him, as he did not follow their gods. They must have spoken against him very strongly, and tried to prevent him from worshipping God in his own way. And Abraham had to leave that country.

He took his family and his flocks, and started wandering, to find the land where he could worship God in peace. He believed God would show him that land.

And that is how the Jewish people began—with Abraham and his family seeking a new home where they could practice their religion. Many, many times in the years since Abraham this same kind of story has been repeated. For instance, we know that America began with the Pilgrims seeking a new home where they could practice their religion freely. We know that in some countries even today there is no freedom of religion. So you see the world is not yet perfect.

Abraham and his family crossed the great river and came toward a place that was then called the Land of Canaan. Many years later it was called Palestine, and now it is called Israel. Abraham was inspired again, when he saw this land; he felt that this was the land God meant for him to dwell in—for him and his family, and for the Jewish people, his descendants.

Abraham was the first Jew

We say that Abraham was the first Jew because he started the Jewish religion with the understanding that there is One God, who is invisible, and who is always everywhere. This is the heart of Judaism.

You may wonder, weren't Adam and Eve also Jews? The Bible tells us the names of their children and their children's children until we come to Abraham. They were the ancestors of the Jews. But Abraham was the first Jew. Judaism began with him.

We say "began," because Judaism

Moses and the Ten Commandments

did not come all in one time. It took centuries for the Jews to discover more and more about God, and we are still learning. Just as you learn new things year after year about the world around you, so our people learn about God in generation after generation.

Moses, the great teacher

And we have great teachers. The greatest teacher after Abraham was Moses. He came hundreds of years later, after Abraham's great-grand-children had fallen into slavery in Egypt.

Moses led them out of slavery, but that was only his first great deed. The second was just as important. He brought them the Torah, the book of the Laws of God. He gave them the first laws, the Ten Commandments, written on tablets of stone.

The first three Commandments are about God.

The first Commandment tells us that God is the Lord who took us out of slavery in Egypt, for people should be free.

The second Commandment tells us that there is only One God and that we cannot make statues or pictures or images of Him, for then we would fall back into idol worship.

The third Commandment tells us not to use God's name in vain. This reminds us that God is vast as the universe, and that we must not try to call upon God for every little thing we want, like idol worshippers who would ask favors and make bargains with their little gods every day.

The other Commandments, as you know, tell us about right and wrong; they tell us what to do and what not to do.

The Sh'ma

Moses also taught the Jews the Sh'ma. Sh'ma is the Hebrew word for "hear," and the name of a prayer. Every time we say the Sh'ma we remind ourselves of the great truth discovered by Abraham, and told to us by Moses, the great truth that is the heart of Judaism. "Hear, O Israel, the Lord our God, the Lord is One."

What we have learned so far

We will always say the Sh'ma, for it calls out the truth from which all of our laws have come. After Abraham and Moses there arose other great teachers, prophets, and rabbis, who helped us to make and to understand these laws.

For until we understood that there is One God, there could not be any hope of people living together in peace in the world. But more and more we understand that there is One God, and that He is the God of all people, everywhere, and that God is always everywhere.

QUESTIONS TO THINK ABOUT

1. Abraham is called the "first Jew." What did he discover to give him this title and what did he do to deserve it?
2. The first three of the Ten Commandments tell us about the most important Jewish ideas about God. Can you tell in your own words what they are?

QUESTIONS TO ASK YOUR PARENTS

1. Ask your parents if they would like to hear you tell one story of how Abraham broke his father's idols. After you have told it to them, ask them to explain the meaning of this story from a parents' point of view.
2. Abraham and Moses were the first teachers who taught the "children of Israel" about God. Ask your parents to tell you how they taught you about God when you were younger.

UNIT TWO

What Judaism Teaches Us About God

CHAPTER III

We Cannot See God But We See His Work

In the old days people believed that God was only in the place where they put his statue. We are told the story of some ancient Romans who were on a ship in a storm. They became terrified that the ship might sink. On the same ship there were some Jews, and they wrapped themselves in their prayer-shawls. Then they prayed to God, and were not afraid.

"It's all right for you," the Romans said to the Jews. "You always carry your God with you in those scrolls of yours. But our god is in Rome, and who knows if we shall reach shore safely to pray to him."

God is everywhere

But of course the Jews knew that God is everywhere, on sea as well as on land.

Even though we cannot see God, we know that He is there. He is everywhere, all the time. We know He is different from people, and from things, because people and things can only be in one place at one time. If you are walking down the street, you are not in your house. If you are sitting in your house, you are not walking down the street.

To know that God is everywhere, makes us feel safe. We do not have to wait for the sun or the moon to comfort us, because we know that God is always there, when it is dark just as when it is light. We know that God is with us wherever we go, in strange places like airplanes, and in everyday places like our cars.

We cannot see God

"But if God is everywhere," we wonder, "why can't we see Him anywhere?"

And the answer is that we cannot see Him, because He has no body or shape or form. That is why the second Commandment forbids our making statues or pictures of God.

Then we ask another question. "If we cannot see Him, how do we know that He is there? Is it possible to know something is there without seeing it?"

And the answer to this is, "Of course it is possible. There are many things in everyday life that we cannot see, yet we know they are there."

We know some things by what they do

We cannot see the wind. But we can see what the wind does. We see sails billow out, and ships moving on the water, and we know that a wind blows. We see the tall grass bend, and the small grass ripple under the wind. We see leaves whirling in circles as they are blown by the wind, and we watch our kites borne high into the sky by the wind. We hear a door slam shut, and we say, "It's the wind." Even if we cannot see or feel the wind we can sometimes smell it by the scents it carries by, the odor of the sea, or the scent of flowers.

But there is something we cannot see or smell, and yet we know it is there. That is the force of gravity.

We can see what the wind does

When a leaf falls to the ground, we know that the force of gravity makes it come down. When we throw a ball into the air, we know it will come back because of the force of gravity.

And there is something in addition to the wind, or the force of gravity, that we cannot see, or feel, or smell, and yet we know it is there. That is love. We cannot see love, and yet we know when we love someone, and we know when someone loves us. We feel a mother's love in just her nearness and in the way she looks at us, and we

We can see the orderliness of the world in large things and small

feel a father's love in his arm around our shoulders. We feel love in the warm and smiling "hello" of a friend.

Love makes us feel warm and safe and happy and good all over. We cannot see love, but we know it is there because of what it does to us and what it can make us do.

That is the nearest feeling to the feeling of God.

We know God by what He does

No one, not even Abraham or Moses or anyone else, has ever seen God. But all of us have seen God's work, everywhere in the world.

Suppose you were travelling in the desert and you passed over vast stretches of sand where there was nothing. And then suddenly there in the middle of the desert stood a palace, with brick on brick placed exactly right. Though you saw no one there, you would say, "This didn't happen by itself. Someone with great intelligence planned it and saw that it was built."

Now think of the earth whirling in the vast deserted regions of space. And think of all the other planets, and the stars. Think of the earth with its oceans and mountains all holding together, and trees on the mountains, and leaves on the trees, and insects on the leaves.

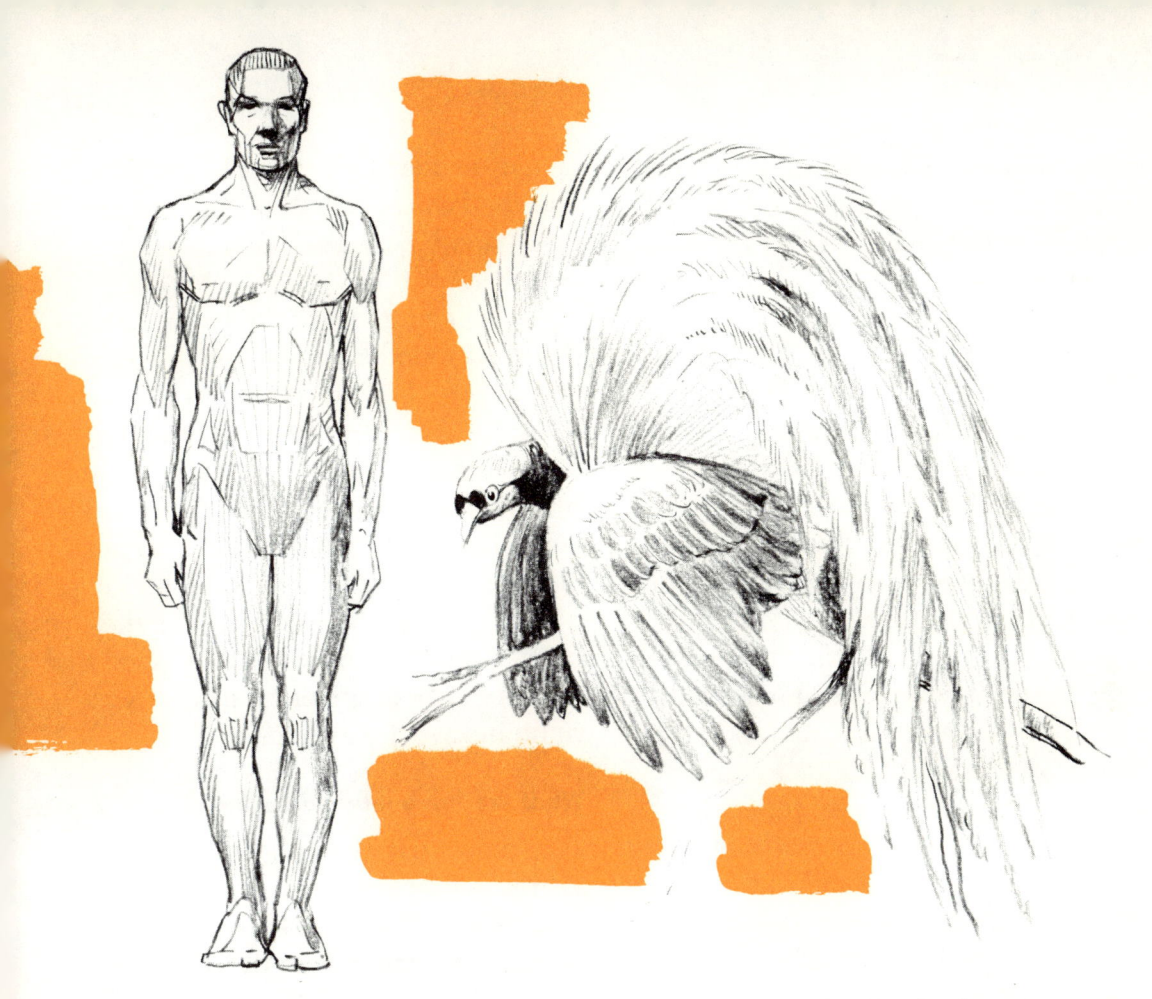

We know there are great laws that hold the universe together. Even in the time of Abraham, men had begun to understand some of these laws of nature. It did not need the powerful microscopes and telescopes and radar of today for men to see and wonder at the orderliness of the universe. And the more we learn about God's laws, the more we marvel.

Each one of us can see for himself the perfection of these laws simply by thinking of his own body. How complicated and how perfect is our body!

The center of life, the heart, is protected by a cage of bones. The different organs in the body produce the chemicals we need to walk and talk and see and think!

And the creation of such a body is not only the creation of a complicated machine. It is the creation of something really beautiful. For the bones and the muscles are then smoothly covered so they make shapes that are pleasing to the eye.

And what is this that we call pleasing? It is a combination of the feelings that come from all these sights and smells and sounds that go through the mind of man. All this thinking and feeling comes to us from God, and it is so wonderful that we can only marvel at it.

We know God by what He teaches us

We understand that these laws of nature are not the only laws created by God. There are laws of how to use nature, so as to bring ourselves the best feelings. They are laws about how to live together.

These are the laws which Judaism sought to discover, beginning with the Ten Commandments and the Torah of Moses.

Indeed through the centuries, Jews have sought to discover not only the laws of astronomy that tell us the path of the stars, and not only the laws of planting crops, and of building houses, and of making machines. Jews have sought not only to discover the laws of nature that help to cure the sick, and the laws of the atom that help us understand how the universe is put together.

Jews have also sought to discover the great moral laws, the laws of right and wrong, the laws of how to behave to each other. For when they understood there is only One God, they understood that there is right and wrong, and that what is right cannot be changed by the favor of a god of the sun, or of the moon. Then they knew that they had to study God's way, to come to understand what was right and what was wrong.

What we have learned so far

We know that there is One God in all the world and that He is always everywhere. Though He never can be seen, yet we know Him by His works. For the whole world that we see tells us that He is there.

QUESTIONS TO THINK ABOUT

1. To understand why we cannot see God, we must understand that there are many things we cannot see but which we know exist. Can you name three of these things mentioned in this chapter and how they prove this idea?

2. God's work can be seen both in th human body and in the universe of stars and planets. Can you explain why this is true?

QUESTIONS TO ASK YOUR PARENTS

1. One way we know that love exists even if we cannot see it is to see what parents and children do when they love each other. Can your parents help you to list some of these things that show this in your family?

2. Rules and laws are the ways in which human beings try to imitate God's order in the world. What kind of rules do your parents expect you to follow so that there can be order in your home?

CHAPTER IV

God Created the World and All Things in It

Did you ever look inside a radio with all its tiny wires and tubes and wonder how a man could ever make it? Did you ever look inside a watch with all its tiny wheels and wonder how a man could ever make it? Did you ever watch a huge jet plane and wonder how people could ever build it?

We build with things we find

When men make radios or even rockets they make them out of things that are already here on earth. The wires of a radio and the walls of a jet plane are made of metal found inside the earth. All the things that go into a watch or a rocket are waiting to be used.

No matter how wonderful the invention, it is made of something already here. When a scientist makes a pill to kill germs he makes it out of things found in nature. When mother bakes a cherry pie, she makes it out of flour and cherries and sugar and things that are already here on earth. And when a carpenter builds a house, he makes it out of things that are made from the earth. Out of nails and wood and stone. When a boy makes a bird-house, he does the same thing.

And when we make something we feel good.

But making things is not creating things.

Everything we *make* is made out of something.

But what is *created* is made out of nothing.

God created the world and everything in it out of nothing!

God created the universe

That is what our forefather Abraham understood. He saw that God created the sun and the moon and the stars and that each moved in its place. He saw that it was foolish to pray to many gods and to stones and to statues and to imagine that the wishes of a little man could change the great plan of the universe. He saw that it was man's task to find out all he could about this plan. For the plan was good.

God created the world and saw that it was good. Even a man, looking around him, could see how wonderful and good the world was.

And where did all this goodness come from? All the beautiful clouds and the stars and the trees and the tiny fishes in the water? We try very hard to think how this happened. And all of our ancestors thought about it, too, and some of their thoughts and their words came into the Bible.

First there was nothing. And then God said, "Let there be light!" And there was light.

Did God speak those words out loud? No, that is not what we mean, for we know that God has no body or mouth. It was a great wish that happened, a wondrous instance of creation.

Have you ever been on the street at the moment when darkness is coming and suddenly all the lights go on? We know that someone pushed a button somewhere. But still we feel that the moment of light is wonderful and magical. First there was darkness on our street, and then there was light!

Then how vast must have been the feeling when light flooded the world!

God's world is full of wonderful things

We see the perfect wonders of nature, right around ourselves. If we look in our own backyard, we see the grass making a soft carpet on the earth; we see vines growing to soften the look of fences and walls; we see flowers of so many different kinds that we can hardly count them. There are flowers as small as snowflakes and flowers that are large and bright like fireballs. We see trees that are wide and leafy with rough bark, and trees that are tall and smooth. Each plant is good and each plant is beautiful.

We know of plants in all the different parts of the earth. We know of flowers that grow in the parched desert and flowers that grow in the cold northlands. Each plant is created exactly right for its own place; and each plant makes its own seeds so that it can go on and on.

And each plant may have a hundred different varieties. There are red roses and yellow roses and even green roses, and each gives seeds of its own kind.

The earth itself is filled with wonderful differences. Our own backyard may be flat, but when we go driving with our parents, we see how many shapes the earth can take. There are rolling hills and valleys, steep cliffs and mountains.

And most of the earth is covered with water—great oceans of water, and lakes in the middle of the land and rivers and brooks. How beautiful the water is! And how beautiful the grass and trees and flowers! And all these different things hold together on the turning globe! What a wonder is creation!

The wonderful variety of creation

So we understand what our forefathers meant when they said God looked at all He had created and saw that it was good.

God looked at every tiniest thing. And He also looked at the big things and saw that they were good.

God created night and day

The earth moved in its great circle around the sun, so that there should be night and day. Of what use was night?

31

Night was for the creatures on earth to sleep, and to build up new energy for their work and play in the daytime.

Each star in the sky had its own path of movement in the universe. And this great and mysterious plan was also good.

God created living creatures

After the creation of the sun and moon and stars and earth, came the creation of living creatures. And what a great number of different creatures! What a great variety!

Fish of a thousand kinds, in the sea and in the rivers. And creatures that came out of the sea, like frogs and lizards. And reptiles that crawled on the earth. And hundreds of creatures that walked and ran on the earth, from the tiny ants to the huge dinosaurs. And birds that walked on the earth and flew in the skies and even swam on the waters. Each according to its kind.

There was the hummingbird, so swift and tiny, hovering like a helicopter. There were the great hawks and eagles. And there were the garden fowl, the chickens and geese.

Each thing lives according to its place and plan

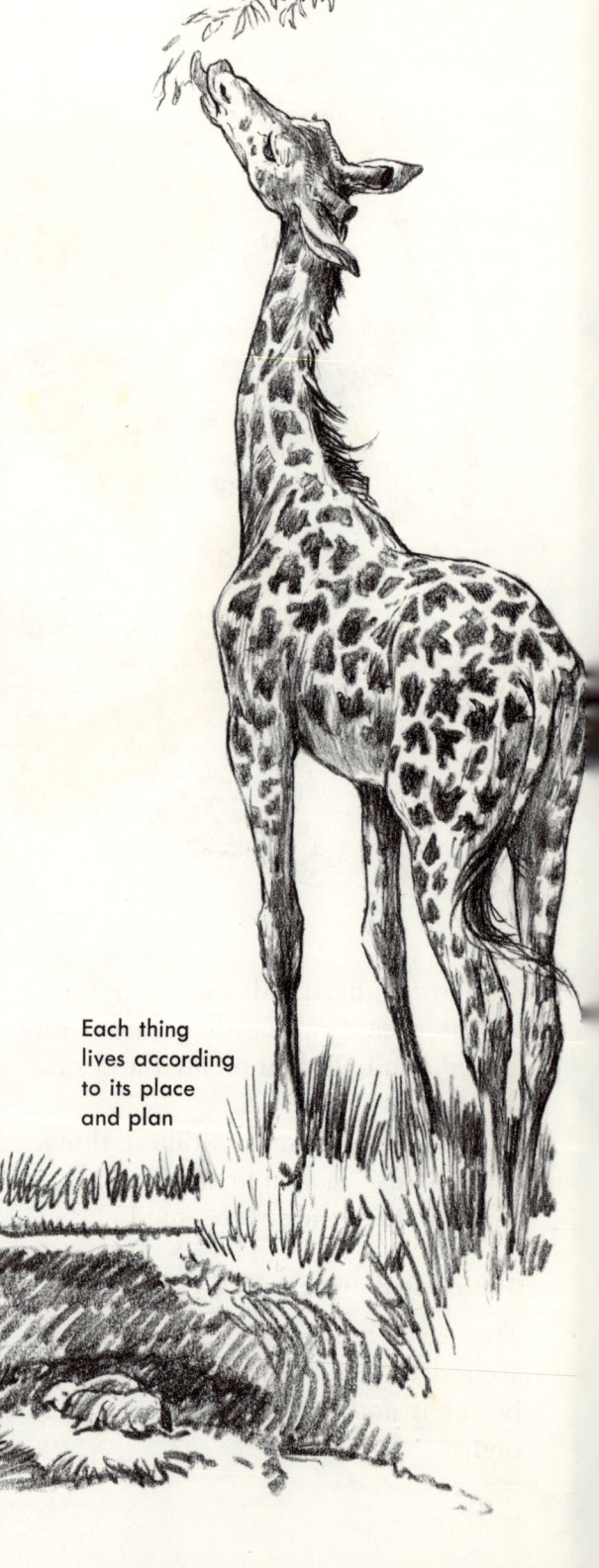

Just as the birds were of many kinds, so were the beasts. We see them in the zoo, brought from all parts of the earth. There is the huge, heavy hippopotamus, wallowing in the water. There is the giraffe, with its long neck. There is the slow snail and the swift deer. There are great wild beasts like lions and tigers, and there are small relatives of them, like cats.

God's creatures have a plan of life

What a great variety there is, in creation! And how wonderful it is that each kind of creature lives according to its own plan!

Think of the comical turtle with its house on its back, and think of the simple worm. Each of these creatures has its own way of living, and though they cannot talk, and cannot write and read, the exact same way of living is known from parents to children and does not change.

The bird knows that it must build a nest in which to place its eggs, and it knows that it must pull worms out of the ground when the eggs open and tiny fledglings are born.

Bees know how to take honey from the flower and how to make honeycombs where they store their treasure. The tiny ant knows how to make complicated cities in the earth. The frog knows how to find its way to water.

Each creature knows what food it should eat. The rabbit eats lettuce and does not eat meat. The kitten likes milk. The bird likes seeds of grain.

All this is the wonder of creation!

Each creature has its own kind of protection, just as the turtle has its shell. The deer has its swiftness. The tiger has its claws. The toad has a muddy color so that his enemies will not see him. Some animals can even change colors, so they can hide.

The Talmud tells us that we may learn lessons from each of God's creatures. Our wise sages said, "God teaches us through the beasts of the earth, and makes us wise through the birds of heaven."

Thus, they said, "If the Torah had not been given to us, we still might have learned many things from the animals. We would have learned the tenth Commandment, "Thou shalt not covet what is thy neighbor's." This means you should not want what belongs to someone else. And we could learn this Commandment from the tiny ants. For if you watch the ants you see that they store up food, yet none of them will ever take what belongs to another.

The cat teaches us cleanliness. The dog teaches us loyalty. The squirrel shows us how wise it is to prepare ahead.

What we have learned so far

The world God made is a good world, and it is filled with wonderful variety. There are thousands of different kinds of plants and animals, yet each belongs to its own kind. The bee knows the ways of the bees; the bear knows the ways of the bears. Each creature has its own purpose, and each creature has its own beauty.

So it is with people, too. Our forefathers saw that there is great variety in nature, but also that there is a great order in nature. Each creature lives by the ways and the laws of nature. Each creature has its own kind. And so each person should know first his own people, and learn the ways of his own kind.

QUESTIONS TO THINK ABOUT

1. In this chapter you were told that you could "create" or make things if you had materials with which to make them. What did you ever "create" or make which gave you the greatest satisfaction?

2. God created a world where nothing existed before. Try to explain in your own words what is meant by "nothing."

QUESTIONS TO ASK YOUR PARENTS

1. We are told in this chapter that "God's plan" can be seen in the life of any animal in the way he first learns to eat, to move, and to protect himself from his enemies. Can your parents help you to explain "God's plan" for human beings in the ways that parents bring up their children in the earliest years?

2. A single small act can show us the wonder of God's creation. For example, pressing a button of an electric switch can light up an entire room. Can you and your parents think of other "small acts" like this which can add to this idea?

CHAPTER V

God Made Order in the World

When we look around us in the world and see how many different kinds of plants and animals there are, we think, how wonderful it is! Yet there is something even more wonderful than all this variety in God's world. It is order.

Did you ever go into a busy railway station? All sorts of people rushing crisscross in different directions. People worrying if they will catch their trains. Mothers worrying that their children will get tangled in the crowd and lost.

Everyone pushes around the information booth. They look at the printed timetable, and then they ask the man in the booth, "Are you sure the train will be on time?"

Your father looks at his watch. Your mother looks at her watch. They both look at the station clock, and then, if all is well, you hear the train thumping into the station and you cry, "There it is! Exactly on time!"

You feel good because it is exactly right. Everything is in order.

We like to have order in our lives

Did you ever wonder how it came about that things are in order? Where did people learn to do things in a regular orderly way instead of pell-mell? Wouldn't it be a complicated world if a train that was supposed to come to New York went to Kansas City instead? And if instead of leaving on Tuesday it left on the Sunday before?

You would be very angry. And also, you might be frightened. You would say, "How can anyone live in a world where things are never the way they are supposed to be!"

But in your life everything is as orderly as people can make it. When you open the back door in the morning, the milk is there.

Where did people learn this idea of order?

They learned it from the world and from the universe, as God made them. God created laws of nature which are so exact that our best scientists, using the best instruments, still have not been able to figure out how things stay so exact. Yet some of these natural laws are so simple that all of us see them working every day without even thinking about them. We take them for granted.

Day, night, the four seasons, are part of God's order

After each day, there is night. We take this for granted. But it is not so simple to make day and night follow each other in a never-ending circle. It means having a sun and a moon in the sky.

We know that things are arranged so that the earth turns like a ball; and in the day one side is toward the sun, and at night the same side is away from the sun.

But how is it that the great ball of the earth and the fiery ball of the sun are arranged in such perfect order that the days and nights follow each other year after year for trillions of

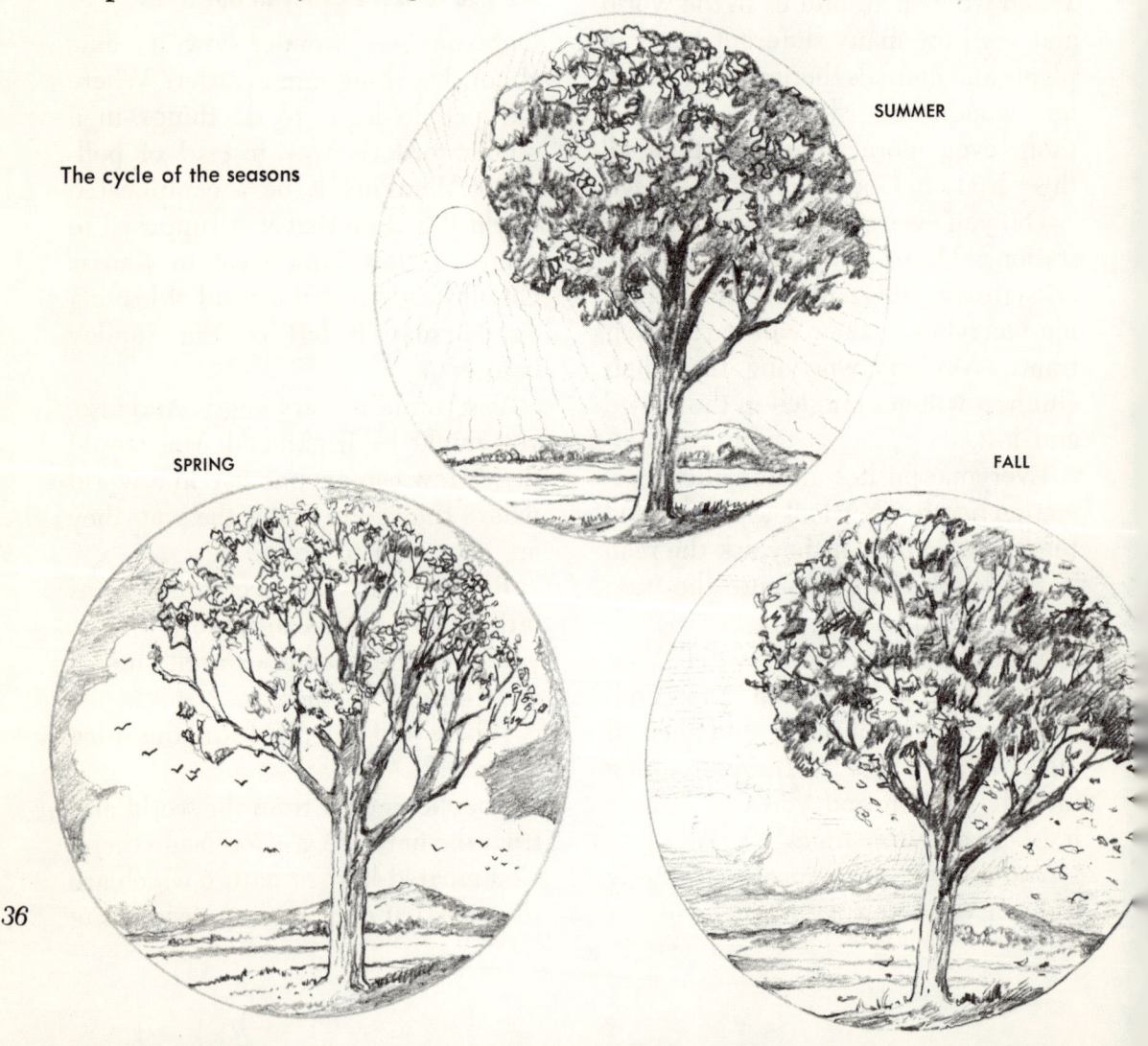

The cycle of the seasons

SUMMER

SPRING

FALL

years without missing a single second?

And just as the days and nights follow each other in perfect order, the seasons of the year come in perfect order. For just as the earth spins like a ball for each day and night, it also travels in a great loop around the sun each year. On different parts of the path we have the four seasons, winter, spring, summer, and fall.

And whenever there is winter and things do not grow, we know for *certain* that spring will come, and the earth will again grow food for us. This is the working of God's law of nature, and it never changes. We know we can trust this law, for it is a law of God's creation.

Long, long ago when Judaism began, our forefathers looked on the wonders of creation and saw how the moon came always in its time, and how each season of the year came always in its time, and they knew that this was eternal and the work of the Eternal.

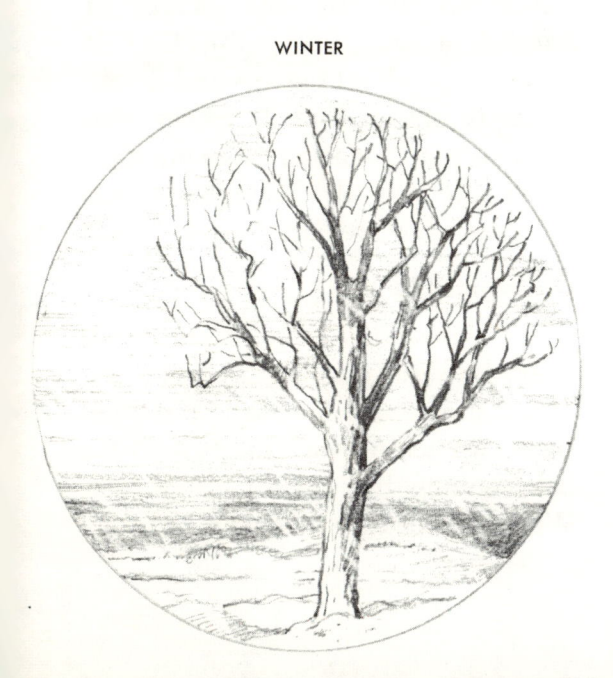

Death is a part of God's order

And they saw another great law in the workings of the Eternal God. They saw that, just as there was light and there was darkness, just as there was summer and there was winter, so there was life and there was death.

Each fall, plants that had been green in the summer became brown, and then, as winter came, they withered and died.

Beautiful roses opened into bloom, gave their fragrance to the air, and then withered and died.

And just as our ancestors saw the life and death of the plants, we too see this. For the order of nature does not change. We breathe the fragrance of the rose, and we enjoy its bright color, but we know that its time will end. It must die.

We know that this is the order of creation.

Birth and growth are part of God's order

And just as it is with plants, so it is with animals. Animals are born, and they give birth to other animals, and in their turn they die. Each animal has its span of life. We know that a dog or a cat will not live as long as a human being.

And as it is with plants and animals, so it is with people. The same law of

WINTER

The cycle of birth, growth, and rebirth

creation holds good for people as it does for all living things.

And so people are born, they grow up, and have children who grow up. The old people die. Judaism teaches us that when a person dies, the life that was in him goes back to God, who makes life and who helps people to stay alive. And when death comes, God takes back to Himself the life that He gave us.

When someone we love dies, we feel sad. We miss that person near us. But our Judaism has taught us that death is a part of life, and our Jewish faith tells us how to express our feelings at such a time so that we will be comforted. When someone we love dies, we say a prayer, a great prayer in praise of God, called the Kaddish. We praise the order of creation. We praise life.

Though we are sad and will miss the one who has died, we know that death is a part of life. We know that this is a law God made and nature must follow. We know that God is good and His laws are good even if we cannot understand all of them.

And so we say the prayer of Kaddish, a hymn that praises God. It says nothing about sadness and death; it simply praises God. It speaks with the heart of Judaism, knowing that death, life and all creation are tied together. They are part of God's order.

Life brings life

Don't we see proof of this in our everyday life? From each plant before it dies comes the seed of another plant. An acorn which drops from the oak contains the seed of a new tree. While the oak may remain standing for many years, the new tree is born and grows.

A living creature leaves new life on earth when it dies, and sometimes it replaces itself many times over. The cat gives us many kittens; the chicken hatches many eggs.

And in the wonderful order of creation, each plant produces its own kind. Dandelions produce dandelions and never buttercups! Chickens produce chickens.

The Bible tells us about these orderly laws of nature. "And God said, 'Let the earth put forth grass, herb yielding seed, and fruit tree bearing fruit after its kind, wherein is the seed thereof.'"

You see this truth each day. When you eat a peach, the seed thereof is inside.

In the great order of the universe, life feeds on life. Plants grow, and as the plants will die, animals feed on the plants. We know that animals also feed on other animals. And people, too, eat the meat of animals. This is in the order of the universe. And our religion teaches us that the order of life and death is sacred. Therefore when we take food and drink from the earth, we do it in a special, sacred way, with blessings and thanks for the food that sustains our life.

What we have learned so far

God made order in the world, making things go on and on, life bringing life, through the wondrous rules of nature. Little by little, mankind is learning about these rules, just as our ancestors began by learning the order of the stars and the moon and the sun and the rules of night and day.

Today our scientists know more about the rules of nature. They know the rules of flight and can send planes into the air. They know about the rules that hold together the tiny atom. They know about the rules that make the earth spin around the sun and the moon spin around the earth, and they can send up satellites like little moons, and also make them spin around the earth.

But the more we discover of the great rules of nature, the more we wonder at the beauty and the wisdom and the order of creation. For the further we can see, the more awesome is the order of the universe.

Our ancestors who began Judaism understood that God made the order of the universe. They saw that God is everywhere, all the time, and that God's law of life is eternal.

We want to make our own life a part of God's way.

QUESTIONS TO THINK ABOUT

1. In what ways is your school as orderly a place as the railroad station described in this chapter?

2. How many things can you name which happen over and over again each day to make us feel that there is order in the world? In each year?

QUESTIONS TO ASK YOUR PARENTS

1. Explain to your parents what you learned in this chapter about the idea that "life brings life." Ask them what this proves to us about God's laws for living things.

2. Judaism teaches us that death is a part of life and that the Kaddish, the prayer for the dead, praises life and the order of creation. Ask your parents how this idea helped them to accept the death of someone they knew.

CHAPTER VI

God Created Man

We know how the tiniest dots of energy, inside an atom, whirl around just like the greatest planets in the sky. The smallest is like the greatest and the greatest is like the smallest. This shows us the amazing wonder of God's plan. Such wonders have been shown us by our scientists, in modern times. Yet in ancient times the Jewish sages understood this very same truth. They did not have microscopes and telescopes. But they had a feeling for God. And they were more like poets than like scientists. So they saw the miracle of God's handiwork in the creation of man.

The Jewish understanding of God teaches us the place of man in God's world. The world was made for man—our Rabbis tell us—and that is why man was the last of God's creatures to be created. Man was the guest of honor, who came to the table to find everything ready for him. God was the host who prepared the tasty food, who set the table, and then led the guest of honor to his seat.

We are told that man was the only creature made by the hand of God. All the other creatures sprang from the word of God. God said, "Let there be birds in the air, and beasts of the field," and there they were. But when the time came to create man, we are told of the "hand of the Creator."

We know this does not mean that God was like a giant being, with huge hands. It is simply a way of making us understand that man is a special kind of creation.

Man has a special way of feeling

With the creatures of the animal world, man shares a wonderful group of senses, more amazing than any of man's own inventions. Man's body is a compact case of instruments for use in living. And beyond this body that God has given him, man has an understanding that is the crown of all creation. For with his special gift of understanding, man can have feelings of love, reverence, beauty and joy.

Like many other creatures, man has

five senses. He can see, hear, smell, taste and touch. These senses help him to see and hear what is happening, and to find his food, and they also act as bodyguards.

But man can do much more than that. He can have special feelings.

As the desert fawn looks carefully about for a prowling lion before venturing out into the open, so a human being in a teeming city looks two ways before crossing a street. But with the same eyes, the human being reads a book that makes his heart glad; with the same eyes, the human being looks out on the beauty of nature, on the delicate frost that covers the trees in winter, on the changing tints of the ocean, and he feels poetry and joy.

The delicate ears of a deer may hear sounds that come in waves too small for the human ear; and yet, just as the deer darts off at the danger-signal of a whisper, so the human being is kept safe by the danger-signals of sounds that he knows, like the toot of a train whistle or the clang of a fire alarm.

But the human being also gets pleasure from sounds he hears, the song of a waterfall, the thrum of the crickets. And the human being can take all the sounds of the world and put them together, and change them, and make them into violin music and orchestra music that sings with the joy of the universe. When we hear such music, everything within us also sings.

Often we watch a cat sniffing her food. In this way, she knows what to eat and what not to eat. And we human beings also make use of our sense of smell, for protection. When mother is about to bake a cake, she cracks an egg and sniffs it. If she doesn't like its smell, she doesn't use it.

But when we catch the scent of the cake baking in the oven, we feel not only a delicious glow in our bodies, but a glow over the entire house.

And sometimes we sniff things simply because we want to.

The rich, sweet smell of honeysuckle is not useful. It does not lead us to food, nor does it warn us of danger. But it tells us that spring has come, and we breathe it because it smells good.

Our sense of taste also serves us in two ways. We can tell when food is bad by its bad taste. Our sense of taste warns us what not to eat.

But our sense of taste serves us in another way, too. It guides us in the creation of cooking. We blend spices into our meat. We flavor our ice cream with the cool tang of peppermint. We enjoy the perfect combination of cream and strawberries.

And our sense of touch also works in two ways. Like any animal, we leap back if we touch a hot piece of iron, or a burning coal. Pain teaches us to stay away from a stinging bee. But how pleasant is the touch of a raindrop on our cheek! What tender feelings we have when we hold in our hand

SIGHT

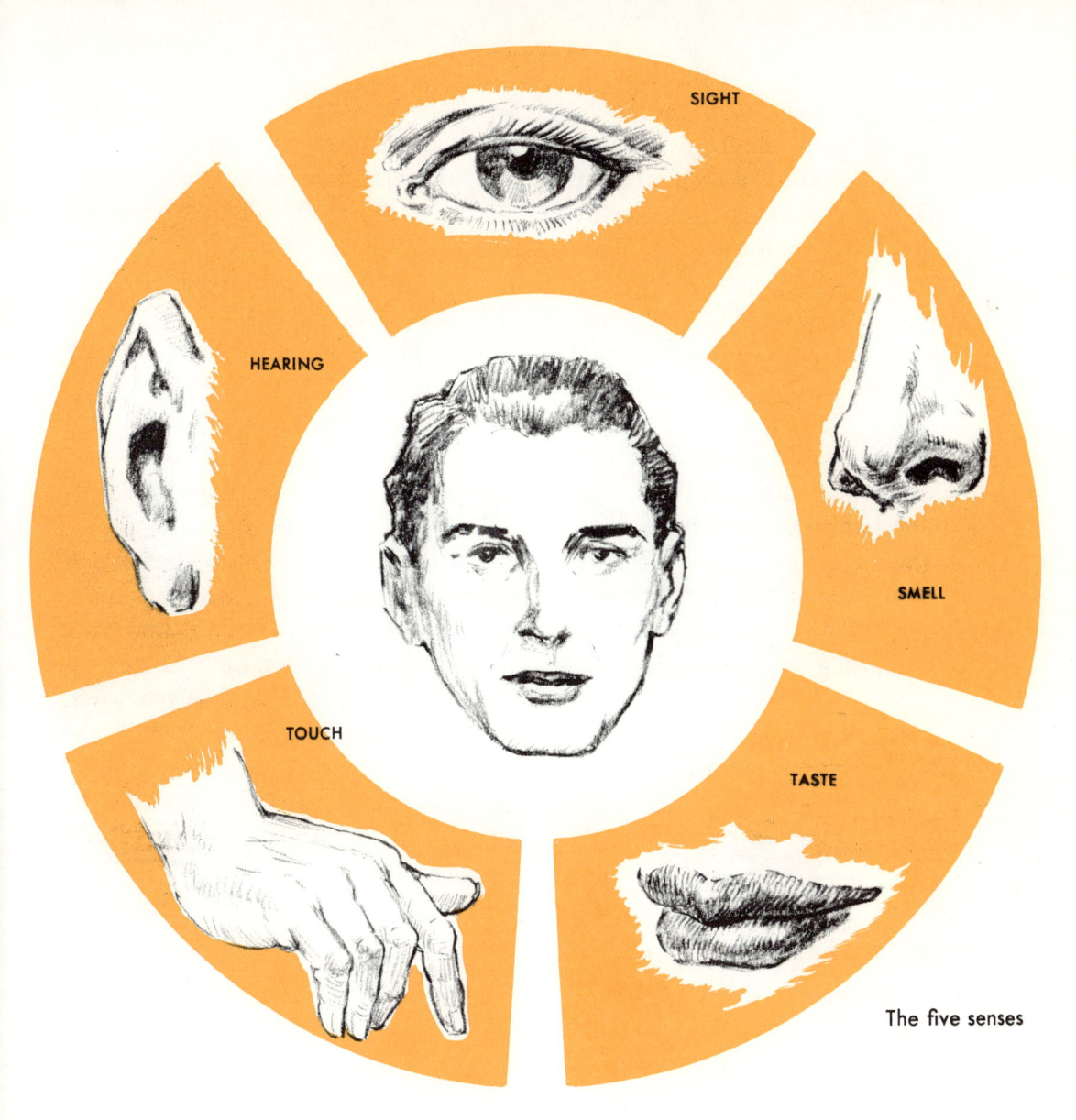

HEARING

SMELL

TOUCH

TASTE

The five senses

the soft, smooth little foot of a baby! What joy and love come with a mother's kiss, a father's hug!

Thus it is that the very same senses which protect and help us in our animal life, also bring us feelings and thoughts that are known only to mankind. And from this we know that man is God's crowning creation.

Though we share our five senses with many of the creatures of the earth, the special gifts of God make these senses serve man in more ways than they serve other animals.

Man has a special kind of body

Our limbs and the organs inside our bodies are marvels that we share with

43

the animal kingdom. With our legs we run, jump, skip, climb, as do the monkey and the cat. Yet our human fancy enables us to invent wonderful dances and sports and games like baseball. Our hands help us to eat, dress, work, play—and with them we can also make music and write words that are far beyond what animals can do.

Inside our bodies, many miracles take place. Our hearts send the life-giving blood through our bodies, as do the hearts of all warm-blooded animals. Our lungs take air into the body and send out the waste. And every breath, like every heartbeat, is a miracle in each human being as it is in each creature on earth.

Our teeth chew food; our stomachs digest it; and our blood carries the chemicals from the food all through our bodies. In this system, too, we are like God's animals.

And like every creature and every plant in the world, we grow in ourselves the seeds of our children. Just as the apple has seeds that make more apples, so do people have in themselves seeds that become people.

All these limbs, organs, and senses work together in a beautiful team, each helping the other. When your mother tells you it's time to get up, your ear hears it, your feet carry you to the bathroom, your hands wash and dress you. You smell the toast and go in for breakfast. Your eyes see by the clock that it is time for you to leave for school.

All the while, your lungs are breathing in air, your heart has been pump-

We show courage in going to school for the first time

ing blood and sending it through your body, and your brain has been receiving and sending messages.

Man has a special character

But besides giving us these complicated bodies, God has given us character.

Part of character, for instance, is courage. Courage helps us face things that frighten us a little, like riding on a plane for the first time, or going to school for the first time, or sticking up for your rights in front of a bully.

God has given us love and understanding, so that we help each other, just as your mother has understanding for you. She watches over you so that you eat properly and don't run out in the rain and catch a cold. God has given us the joy of love, between parent and child, husband and wife, brothers and sisters, friend and friend. He has given us the joy of beauty, so that we feel happier when we see the colors of a butterfly's wing, or hear the music of a waterfall.

What we have learned so far

God gave people many wonderful feelings that He did not give to the other creatures of the earth. What is man, then? Is he only a kind of animal, or is he something closer to God? The Bible gives us the answer when it says that man was created "in the image of God."

Like the animal, man needs food and drink. He eats and sleeps. His senses help him to protect himself. His limbs and organs work together in a marvelous way.

But man is much more than the animals. For God gave him special gifts, gifts of heart and mind. God made man special by putting a little of Himself into each of us. This is what the Bible means when it tells us that man is made "in the image of God."

QUESTIONS TO THINK ABOUT

1. How does the story of creation tell us that man is the most important of God's creatures?
2. Why is the human body sometimes described as a place of "many miracles"?

QUESTIONS TO ASK YOUR PARENTS

1. Beyond the miracles of the human body, God gave man the power to "feel love and beauty and joy." Ask your parents to explain why these can be considered even greater "miracles."
2. How can we use our senses to bring us these feelings so that we may appreciate the world which God created for man? Tell your parents some of the ways described in this chapter and see if you can add other examples of your own.

CHAPTER VII

God Gave Man Special Gifts

When we have a pet dog, we often say, "He is almost human! He understands everything that is said to him!" Because animals have senses and organs similar to ours, we often say they are almost like human beings. They run on their legs, see with their eyes, hear with their ears—often better than we do.

Indeed pets of many kinds can learn to understand simple things, like bringing back a ball or jumping through a hoop. Some creatures can even learn to make the sounds of human words, as parrots do. So we often forget the very great differences that there are between man and all other creatures.

We all know the main difference. It is in thinking and in telling our thoughts.

Animals do not think and speak

When a parrot says, "Polly wants a cracker," is the parrot really doing the same thing as when you say, "Mom, I'm hungry!"?

Before we answer, let us think of some of the things we can do with a machine. We can easily make a machine that plays a record and says, "Mom, I'm hungry," every time someone walks across an electric eye. This is the same as Polly saying, "Polly wants a cracker" every time a person walks into sight.

Our first answer is that the machinery of human life can be found in animals, too. But the mind that uses that machinery is found only in man. For instance, a child can learn not to bother mother if she is busy or not feeling well, but instead to go and get some milk and crackers in the kitchen. A parrot can't judge when someone is tired or not feeling well.

When a dog is sick and we take him to a veterinarian, the dog can't tell what is wrong and where it hurts. But when a person is sick, the doctor asks, "Were does it hurt?" and the person answers, "My throat hurts." The doctor asks, "All the time, or only when you swallow?" "Only when I swallow." "Does it hurt anywhere else?"

And from these questions and answers, the doctor soon knows what is wrong.

The power to think and speak are special gifts that God gave to man.

We sometimes imagine that certain animals also have the power to think. Animals can think and feel and even express themselves, but only in a very limited way.

And some animals, like dolphins, seem to be able to think and even talk very much the way human beings can.

However, the greater and wider world of thinking and creating is beyond the brains of almost all animals, even the brightest ones like the dolphins. Only man can think long thoughts, dream, write and read and tell his knowledge to other people in other places.

Machines do not think

You have heard about "thinking machines." These machines can add and multiply and do very hard problems in mathematics much more quickly than people can do them. But these machines are not really "thinking." Everything they do has been thought out and put into them by men on pieces of tape or on punch-cards. The machine only sorts out these orders and quickly puts them together.

Thinking helps man do remarkable things

Because man can think, man can do many things for which his body was not made. Without wings, he can fly

A sick person can tell a doctor where he feels pain: an animal cannot

47

higher than the eagle. Though he cannot run as fast as the deer, he can easily pass the deer in an automobile or in a train. Though his body is not made to stay under water very long, he can stay under for hours with oxygen tanks.

He can dig deeper than the mole. He is stronger than the lion because he can fight the lion with bullets.

From the first piece of stone that was used as a hammer to the huge cranes that help build skyscrapers, man has kept on making tools with which to build homes, make clothing and furniture, with which to grow food and cook it, with which to carry things and protect himself from attack. An animal, however, cannot make even a single tool.

Man also makes tools to learn, to satisfy his curiosity. With his microscopes, he can see the tiniest living cell. He can see far into space and to distant planets with his telescopes. With these two tools, man can see everything from the shape of snowflakes to the canals on Mars.

With tools he can do things more and more easily. Imagine digging out a tunnel with a shovel instead of a machine! But also, because man can think and make tools, he can change the way he lives.

An animal can live only where its own kind of food can be found. Man can live in the desert if he wants to and bring food there. Only animals like polar bears can live in the arctic. But man can make warm clothing for himself and live there, too. He can heat his home.

Man can make light where there is dark; he can make heat where there is cold; he can make cold where there is too much heat.

Because he can think, man can protect himself from disease and make his life longer. Doctors can watch people who have a certain sickness. By thinking and using microscopes and other wonderful tools, they can find the germ that causes the sickness. Then they can make medicines to stop it. That is how a vaccine was found to protect us from polio, which used to cripple so many of us.

Man knows how to enjoy himself

Man's mind makes him different from animals in still other ways. When an animal has eaten his fill, he does not read books or listen to music or go to the movies. He does not play chess. An animal is not interested in anything beyond the needs of life. But man's true life begins only after he has satisfied those simple needs. Then he invents, he explores. He makes paintings and sculptures, he writes poems, he makes music, and he thinks about God.

Man is helped in his thinking by his memory. Animals, too, have memories. An animal can remember the smell of the place where he lives; he can

ANIMAL COMMUNICATION   HUMAN COMMUNICATION

remember which way he must go to get home; he can remember his friends.

But only man can remember what someone said many years ago, or what he read in a book.

In the same way that they have only tiny memories as compared to people, animals have only a very small range of sound. Each animal can make a few sounds. Horses neigh, birds sing, cows moo, but they cannot speak.

Sometimes their sounds are signals. A dog's bark can sound happy when his master comes home. A cat hears the mew of her kittens and runs to them. But the kitten cannot tell exactly what it wants. Does it want milk? Does it want to play? Is it sick?

People, on the other hand, can tell others exactly what they want and what they remember and what they think. And only people can tell each other these things in letters, newspapers and books. And only people can make their messages last, instead of vanishing into thin air.

Because man is able to think, his life is altogether different from that of

49

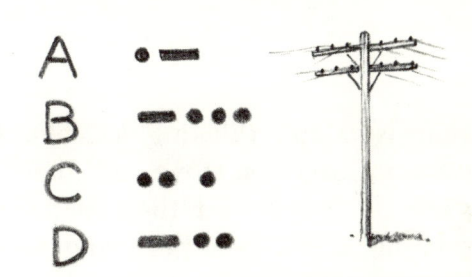

Man's thinking has led to progress in learning

animals. Man's thinking led him to carve messages on stone, and then to write on paper, and then to invent printing, and typewriters, and tape-recorders, and cameras.

In cave-pictures of stone-age men, we also see pictures of animals, such as horses and dogs. Since the stone age, man has learned to send rockets into outer space, but the dog and the horse, like other animals, have not changed their lives.

Because of God's special gift to man, the gift of the human mind, we can change the way we live, and we can share our new ideas, and we can make them last for people not yet born.

People learn from each other

Jews who lived thousands of years ago wrote their ideas and their laws into great books like the Bible and the Talmud. And today we are helped by their thinking.

Arithmetic was discovered many thousands of years ago. We do not have to discover it for ourselves. We only have to learn what others have already figured out for us.

Each man does not have to do everything for himself. A bear has to find his own food and his own lair. But a man who spends his time making music can buy his food at the supermarket and live in a house built by many other men working together.

One man has made the design; another has bought the machinery to dig the foundation; others have put up the walls; and still others have put in the plumbing and the electricity.

It is true that there are some creatures in the world, like ants, who work together. Yet from century to century they do everything the same way.

But man changes. The son learns what his father did, and tries to do it in a better way, more easily, more usefully. And the father is proud when the son carries his work further.

"In the image of God"

Man is indeed a very special creation. Man not only thinks, but feels in a special way. He feels the wonders of God's universe. He feels this, because God put a little of Himself into each of us. This is the most wonderful gift of all, this divine gift.

This tiny bit of God in each of us helps us in something that no other creature can understand, something even more important than inventing tools and making life better. This tiny bit of God helps us understand the difference between right and wrong.

Only man can think about right and wrong.

This ability is so wonderful that it is holy, for it comes closest to what is God. Because every person is made "in the image of God" and has the power to know right from wrong, every human being is holy. You and

51

every other person share in this holiness.

Because we are made "in the image of God" we can be God's partners or helpers. We can make the world better by understanding that each person has a spark of God in him, and that we must treat each person and all people with respect for that spark in them, which is holy.

What we have learned so far

God gave man special gifts that make him different from all other creatures; He gave man the power to think, to speak, to remember, and to share. But above all, He gave man the power to feel the joys and sorrows of the spirit and to know right from wrong. Thus, He made man in His own image.

QUESTIONS TO THINK ABOUT

1. How many things can you think of which human beings can do but which animals cannot do?
2. One of the gratest gifts given to man is the power to put his thoughts into words. Why is this true?

QUESTIONS TO ASK YOUR PARENTS

1. Why do we say that man can act as if he were God's "partner" in continuing the work of creation? How can parents do this?
2. The Bible tells us that "man is made in the image of God." Explain this idea to your parents and ask if they can give you their ideas about this.

With animals "might makes right"

CHAPTER VIII

God in History

An animal does not worry about the difference between right and wrong, between fair and unfair. When it is thirsty it drinks, and when it is hungry it eats. With the animal "might makes right."

Yet even an animal can be taught to wait its turn before it drinks or eats. A dog can even be taught not to eat when its food is in front of it, until his master gives him the signal to go ahead.

But if a dog, or a hen, or a kitten waits its turn to feed, that does not mean the animal has learned politeness. First, it means that the animal lets other animals go first because they are stronger.

And if a dog learns to wait for a signal from his master before he eats, it only means he has learned to do this by a system of rewards. He knows that if he obeys his master he will get good things.

Often, in the life of people, too, it looks as though the animal rule is the only thing that counts, that the stronger person wins the good things.

And when we try to live not like animals but by rules of right and wrong, fair and unfair, instead of by who is stronger, it often seems that the rules don't work. We see times when the good person suffers all kinds of trouble and pain.

But we say, "In the end, over a long time, the good person will be rewarded."

We say this because we see it happen in our everyday lives. We see that the wicked and selfish people who may seem to have good things and success at first, are not so happy as time goes on. And we also see things even out in the lives of entire nations.

There are laws for nations

The lives of nations stretch over long centuries of history. And to understand a little more of the meaning of God's mysterious world, we look at the record of how things have worked out not only in the lives of certain people, but in the whole stretch of human history.

For the life of one person is only a tiny part of human history. And the history of all the people in the world is only a tiny part of the working out of God's universe.

We know that there is only one God for the universe and the world and all the nations in the world and each person in each nation.

God made the laws which nature and people and nations must follow. He is the judge when His laws are broken—whether by people or by nations.

Our people always knew this. They believed that the nations which live by God's laws, and try to make life better for their people and for their neighbor nations will live on.

Our people believed that the nations that are greedy and are not fair to their neighbor nations will ultimately destroy themselves, just as people do.

Nations that do not obey God's law of justice and love and freedom and peace come to trouble in the end. Nations that do not respect the rights of each person in the end grow a poison in themselves which destroys them.

We can see this in history.

The nearest example to our lives is the example of Hitler's Germany. Under the rule of Hitler and his Nazis, Germany became greedy and wanted to possess the land of other nations and to make slaves of other people. They caused much suffering in the world, including the murder of six million Jews.

But in the end they were beaten. Their cities were smashed and they suffered miserably. Hitler killed himself and Germany was cut in two.

This has happened again and again in history. When the ancient Greeks tried to rule other nations, they were in the end destroyed and left small and poor. When the Romans tried to rule the world of their time, and enslave other people, they too ended in defeat and misery.

Nations have special talents

In the working out of history, there is another way in which nations are like people. Some nations seem to have a talent for a special task.

Just as one child may have a gift for arithmetic, another for geography, another for sports, and another for music, so it is with nations. The Greeks had a talent for beauty. They made statues which gladdened the eyes and hearts of all who looked on them. They wrote poems and plays which we still read today. They built temples that were models of design and workmanship.

After the Greeks, the Romans rose to power. Their special talent was for organizing. They made laws which are models of the laws of many countries today. They built roads on which to travel. They organized groups of soldiers to fight together as one man.

When we ask what kind of special talents do nations have in modern times, we can look at our own country and see how the American talent for making machinery has changed the way people live. Everyone lives more comfortably because of the American idea of making things cheaper by making them with machines.

The Jews had a talent for religion

The Jews, too, had a special talent as a people. Their gift was for understanding about God. The gift for religion first showed itself among the ancient Hebrews.

Living among people who believed in many gods, Abraham was the first to understand there is One God for all the world. He taught this idea to his son, Isaac, and Isaac taught this to his son, Jacob. So Abraham, Isaac and

Different nations have made different contributions

Jacob became the three "fathers," or patriarchs, of the Jewish people who believed in One God. That is why our prayers often say, "God of Abraham, Isaac and Jacob."

Because the patriarchs and the Jewish people after them had a special talent for religion, they tried to discover and understand the great rules of God's universe. They tried to understand how people should treat each other, how they should live, so as to be in harmony with God's rules.

It was as though they were listening with all their might. And that is why the Jewish prophets so often said that God told them what was right and what was wrong.

The chosen people

The first such great prophet was Moses, who brought the Jews the Ten Commandments and the great laws that followed.

Why were these Commandments given by God to the Jews instead of to other people? A story of the Talmud tells us why the Jews were chosen from all the seventy nations on earth, to receive God's laws.

The story says that one after another the nations were asked to receive the Law, so that they might not afterwards complain, "We were never asked! We would have accepted it!" God asked each one, and each one said, "No, thank you," because it was too hard to keep the Law.

For example, the story tells us, the Lord revealed Himself to the people

The Bible tells of the early life of our people

of Esau, and they asked, "What is written in the Law?"

"Thou shalt not kill," they were told.

"No, thank you!" they said, "we live by the sword!"

Then the Lord revealed Himself to the children of Ishmael and said, "Will you receive the Law?"

"What is written in it?" they asked.

And He said, "Thou shalt not steal."

"No, thank you!" they said.

And so it was with all other people, until the Lord came to Israel. The Hebrews said, "All that the Lord has said, we will do, and we will obey."

And so, because the Jews chose to receive God's laws, they felt that God had chosen them too, and they called themselves the "chosen people." This did not mean they were chosen for special *favors*. It meant they were chosen for special *duties*. It was their duty to live in the right way, to be an example in teaching the world the right way to live. Their whole history would be an example of what is right and what is wrong.

That is why Jewish history and Jewish religion are closely tied together. Our Bible is our holy book, the book of our religion. Yet, it is also our great history book. For it tells about the early life of our people, about our patriarchs, our kings, and our prophets.

It tells how Abraham made a covenant with God, who led him to the land where he might worship freely, and said to him, "Unto thy seed will I give this land."

57

Freedom from slavery

But to know the worth of freedom, the Jews had to know what it was to be slaves. And the Bible tells us how the descendants of Abraham became slaves in Egypt, and then were led out to freedom by Moses. They were freed from slavery to a mortal ruler. They were free to discover and live by God's laws.

So great was this truth, so important was this moment, that we are reminded of it every time we hear the Kiddush on Sabbath and on the holidays, for with every Kiddush we thank God for having taken us out of slavery in Egypt.

And once each year we have the great holiday of Passover when we celebrate the great truth that we learned—that we must live not by man's rule, but by God's law.

Indeed, our daily prayers also remind us of this great event, for at the end of the Sh'ma we repeat: "I am the Lord, your God, who brought you out of the land of Egypt."

But like all other people the Jews are not perfect, and time and again in our history we have grown careless and fallen away from God's laws. The Bible tells of such times, when the prophets warned and begged the Jews to return to God's laws. There were Jewish kings who were unfair and wicked. There were times when the rich oppressed the poor.

And finally mighty nations punished our people and drove them out of their land.

This happened twice. The first time Jerusalem was destroyed, and our people were driven into exile to Babylonia. The second time, hundreds

At the Passover Seder we remind ourselves of our liberation from Egypt

of years after they had come back from Babylonia, Jerusalem was again destroyed and the Jews were scattered all over the world.

Yet, because there were always some Jews who held together and kept God's laws, the Jewish people live on while the Babylonians and the Romans who destroyed Jerusalem no longer exist as nations.

What we have learned so far

Our sages tell us that as long as we obey and teach God's law, we shall live on and be of importance as a people. As long as we strive for justice and freedom and peace, as long as we feel brotherhood and love for mankind, our people will live on.

As long as we remember there is only One God, and seek to understand and live by His laws, the Jewish people will live on and on.

QUESTIONS TO THINK ABOUT

1. We know that animals can be trained by giving them a reward when they do what we ask them and punish them when they don't do it. Should children be trained in the same way? Explain the reasons for your answer.
2. The most important event in Jewish history, to judge from our prayers, is the freeing of the Jews from slavery in Egypt. Why should this be so?

QUESTIONS TO ASK YOUR PARENTS

1. Jews think of themselves as a chosen people because they chose to obey God's laws as an example to other peoples. Ask your parents if other peoples also consider themselves "chosen" for any reason.
2. We are told that God judges nations as well as people. Ask your parents how this explains the history of ancient Greece and Rome as well as that of the people of Israel.

CHAPTER IX

God Is Different from People

In the world, many things can be compared to each other, though they are not exactly alike. But by comparing them we know them better. We can compare roses and daisies. Both grow out of the earth; both have stems, leaves and petals. But they have different colors, different shapes, different perfumes. And so we know which is a rose and which is a daisy.

In the same way we can compare animals. Let us take camels and horses. Both have four feet and a head and ears and eyes and noses, and both serve man by carrying burdens on their backs. Yet the camels have humps and horses don't. And there are many other ways in which we can tell them apart.

In the same way we can compare different kinds of fruit. Some of them belong to the same "family." Oranges, lemons and grapefruit, for example, grow in the same part of the world from the same kind of soil, and on trees that look quite alike. But they have different shapes, different skins, different tastes.

The same may be said for people. They all have minds and spirits; all have the same kind of bodies, but individuals have different personalities, different interests, and different colored skins. Yet they all feel love, anger, fear. They all want to protect their families. They all want to know God.

God is unique

But when we reach the idea of God, we can no longer make comparisons. We need at least *two* of something in order to compare. And there is only One God.

Only God creates life out of nothing. Man can plant a seed to grow a tree. He can get wood from the tree and build a house from the wood. But he cannot *make the seed* which he plants, to start the tree. He is not like God. Man cannot create out of nothing the seed that is the beginning of life.

A man can build large hatcheries for chicks. He can take hens' eggs and put the eggs into hatcheries and get thousands of chicks. He can control the heat that makes the eggs hatch. But the secret of life is already inside the egg. Only God can start the secret of life.

So no matter what wonders man performs, he cannot possibly be compared to God. Man can only help God's work after the miracle of creation has already taken place. Man can take God's seed and plant it and water it. He can warm the egg and feed the chick and help it grow.

But the great act of creation belongs to God alone.

God has no body or form

We know that in the old days people tried to imagine what God is like. They pictured God in human or animal form. But the Jewish sages, long, long ago saw how wrong this was.

The sages said, "We can see people, but we cannot see God. We can see people because we see their bodies; we cannot see God because He has no body. He has no shape or form."

Our Jewish sages said, "We can make pictures of people and of animals because they have bodies and we can see them. But because God has no body, we cannot make pictures of Him."

You may wonder, since God has no body, why does the Bible speak of

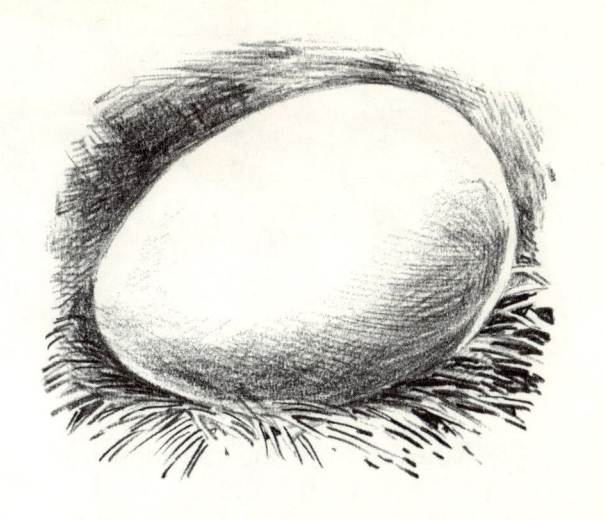

An egg hatches a chick only if the secret of life is within it

"the hand of God" or "the mouth of God."

And the answer is, that the Bible was written for people in words they can understand. Sometimes this language is like poetry. It speaks to our imagination instead of to our ordinary sense.

We use such language in many ways. We say the sun smiles on the earth, yet we know the sun has no face or mouth and does not really smile.

We speak of golden leaves dancing in the breeze. We know that leaves do not have feet and cannot dance. This is just a poetic way of talking.

In the same poetic way we understand that the "hand of God" really means the *work* of God, and the "mouth of God" really means the *teaching* of God that comes into our minds and hearts.

God is neither male nor female

In ancient times when people tried to make pictures of gods, they made men-gods and women-gods. Just as people are either male or female, they thought that gods should be male and female. But we know now that God cannot be male or female, because God has no body. We speak of God as "Him" only because we speak in the ordinary language of people.

Because God has no body, God does not eat or drink or sleep. And all the stories about foods of the gods, all the stories about things happening while the gods slept, are, of course, only stories.

God does not change

We cannot compare people to God. For we change from the moment we are born. When you were a baby you could not walk. When you learned to walk you could not yet read. When you grow old, your hair will turn gray.

But God is always the same. He does not change.

God is present in all the forms of nature

It is only the *way* people think about God, that may change. In ancient times, people thought about God as a special kind of person. But now we know that even when people thought about God as a person, God was the same as always, without shape or form, without beginning or end.

Only God is always everywhere

People can only be in one place at one time. One of our sages, Rabbi Phineas, said, "If an earthly king is in his bedchamber, he is not in his dining room, and vice versa. But God fills the upper and the lower regions at one and the same time. For it is said, in the Bible, 'Do I not fill heaven and earth?'"

God is everywhere all the time. He is above us and around us and inside us, too—all the time. And at the same time he is in all the other people in the world, too.

It is not always easy for people to understand how God can be so great as to fill the universe and so small as to be inside the egg of the smallest ant. Our sages tried to explain this with a story: A Samaritan asked Rabbi Meir, "How is it possible that He of whom it is written, 'Do I not fill heaven and earth?' should have spoken to Moses between the two staves of the ark?"

Then Rabbi Meir said, "Bring me a magnifying mirror." When the Samaritan brought it, Rabbi Meir said, "Look at yourself in the mirror." The Samaritan did so, and saw his face so large that he could see every pore of his skin. Then Rabbi Meir said, "Bring me a mirror that makes things smaller." The Samaritan did so and saw his face made very small. Then Rabbi Meir said, "If you, a mortal man of flesh and blood, can change from large to small without changing your body, how much more can God!"

Only God is eternal

Just as God is everywhere, He is eternal. God was not born and will not die. He always was and always will be.

People are not like that. People are born, and they die. A hundred years ago you were not here. But God was always here and will always be here and everywhere.

Only God can do everything

People can do many things, but they cannot do everything. God can do everything. People can turn on electric lights, but they cannot turn on the sun, and they cannot make the sun set.

Only God knows everything

People can learn and know very much, but they cannot know everything. Even if all the things that all the people of the world know were put together in a super-encyclopedia, it would only be the beginning of man's knowledge.

No one person can possibly know everything, even about one science. No doctor knows all about medicine, for there are specialists in every part of medicine. No musician knows all the music in the world. No teacher has read all the books in the world.

But God has all the knowledge that exists. All living things are His creation. He knows them each and all. All nature is His creation. He knows each blade of grass. All the knowledge that we discover is knowledge that comes from God.

What we have learned so far

So we understand, with the help of all the Jewish prophets and sages, that God is perfect, and only God is perfect. Each person can try to learn more and to do better things, but no person can be perfect.

But God is altogether different, because only He is perfect.

QUESTIONS TO THINK ABOUT

1. When people try to describe God in language that also describes human beings, we say that it is like using the language of poetry. Can you give an example from this chapter or from your own mind?

2. Why is the second Commandment explained to mean that pictures or statues should not be used to decorate a synagogue?

QUESTIONS TO ASK YOUR PARENTS

1. Ask your parents to explain how God can be everywhere at the same time. Tell them how Rabbi Meir explained this idea through the use of a magnifying mirror.

2. Because we believe that God knows everything and can do everything, we say that God is perfect. Ask your parents whether a person should also try to be perfect. Why?

CHAPTER X

We Cannot Know Everything About God

In these times, when each day scientists are finding out new wonders of God's universe, it is hard for men to remember that they cannot ever know everything. Sometimes a man of great power arises and says, "There is no God. I can rule the world. I can command life and death." Such men have brought great wars upon the world. But in the end they too die, knowing that even the greatest human power is as nothing.

Jewish wisdom saw this long ago. In the time when our Talmud was being written, there were kings on earth who believed themselves to be like God. The Roman Emperor, Hadrian, was one of those.

After returning from his conquests, the Talmud tells us, Hadrian called all his courtiers together and said, "Now I demand that you worship me as God."

One of his courtiers, hearing this, said: "Please sire, help me in my hour of need."

"What troubles you?" asked Emperor Hadrian.

"Sire, I have a ship that carries all I possess in the world. It is becalmed, three miles out at sea."

"That is nothing," Hadrian said. "I will send out a fleet, to rescue it."

"Why trouble to send the fleet?" asked the courtier. "Since you are God, only send a little puff of wind."

By such little stories, Jewish sages reminded people that human beings are very small even when they think they are very big, and that they cannot know how to do everything, for only God has perfect knowledge.

The world is mysterious to us

No matter how much we find out, we cannot know everything about the world, about people, about God. The simplest mysteries are the greatest mysteries to us.

We can watch and observe the ways of God. We can see that a chicken's egg hatches in three weeks, and a duck's egg in four. But we don't know why.

There is an odd little mystery about the food we eat. We may eat green peas and yellow corn, red strawberries and whitefish. But why is it that none of the natural foods we find are blue? Even blueberries are not really blue. If you look at their color, you will find they are more purple than blue. How does it happen that there is no sky-blue vegetable? We don't know.

And there are wonders in the world that we cannot explain. How does it happen that hot springs of water suddenly appear in the freezing regions of the Arctic?

How does it happen that birds can find their way each year, at their migration time, from one half of the world to the other? How does it happen that the salmon always finds its way home to its own stream after going out into the ocean?

We are mysterious to ourselves

There are little mysteries and great mysteries about human beings that we cannot solve. Here is a little one: Why do some people like raspberry jam while others like grape jam? If people's bodies are made on the same plan, why don't they all like the taste of the same foods?

Suppose three people watch a sunset over a lake. One may write a poem about it, and the second may want to paint a picture of it, and the third person may say, "It's getting chilly. Let's go indoors."

We cannot explain why God allows fires and floods and earthquakes to happen

"Oh," you say, "that is because each person has a different character." But that is only another way of asking the same question. That is part of the mystery.

God's ways are mysterious

We simply cannot know the answers to all questions. Our wisest men, our parents, our teachers, our rabbis, our psychologists and our other scientists cannot answer them all. Just as we cannot know everything about the universe, or even about its smallest creatures, so we cannot know everything about God. That is one of the things we must know—that we cannot know everything.

It would, of course, be very interesting to know why one man wants to paint a picture of the sunset while his friend only feels chilly. It would be equally interesting to know why one child likes strawberry jam and another likes plum jelly. But in the end, it does not matter very much. There are, however, other questions, which are much more important.

For we know that in life there are often sorrows and accidents which do not seem right to us. We cannot explain why God allows fires and floods and earthquakes to happen. We cannot explain why some people go through life blind or deaf or crippled. Before such mysteries, we can only stop and say, "This is beyond the limit of knowledge that God has given us."

There are some things we do know

Yet, though we cannot know the answers to the great mysteries of life, there are some things that we do know. We know that God is One, and that He created the world and everything in it. We know that He created man in His own image, though imperfect. We know that He helps man, and that He rules the world and the nations in some vast plan. We know that God is different from people, for He alone is perfection.

Although God is only One, He has many names. And these names teach us many things. They teach us how our people thought and felt about God.

The Hebrew name for God is *El* or *Elohim*.

Our people also call God by the Hebrew word, *Adonai*, which means "my Lord."

In our prayers we often speak of God as "The Holy One, Blessed Be He."

We also speak of "the Almighty," which in Hebrew is *Shaddai*. This is the word that appears on the Mezuzah.

And we speak of Him as "the Rock," as in the *Rock of Ages*. This is because a rock is strong and solid and because we see it is something everlasting.

Because the idea of God is holy, we do not want to use the name of God in everyday ways. And so, to avoid using the name of God too easily, many people will say, *Ha-Shem* or "the Name."

We call God "Heavenly Father," because He loves us as a human father loves and cares for his children.

In ancient times, the name of God was considered to be so holy that only the High Priest could speak it. On Yom Kippur, the High Priest would enter the Holy of Holies of the Temple, which was the inner, forbidden chamber. There he would pronounce the wonderful Name of God, in Hebrew, to call on Him on the great day of repentance.

Did this mean that God has a secret name, like some word of magic? Some people believed so, but wise people know that God is nameless. Silence can call on God. Music can call on God.

Even though we cannot know everything about God, we can know how He wants us to live. He has given us laws.

God tells us how to live

One of these laws reminds us every week that creation is holy. This is the fourth Commandment, which says, "Remember the Sabbath day, to keep it holy."

It reminds us that God rested on the seventh day from His work of creation. Therefore the seventh day is a day of Godly rest, a day of prayer and joy.

It is a holy day to remind us that people are holy; this makes us feel closer to God. Sabbath is a day when not only man but his beasts of the field shall rest, to remind us that in God's law all creatures have a right to rest.

When we begin to understand the laws of right and wrong, we begin to understand that we must treat all people as equals, if we would do right.

We know that our feelings of fairness and justice are Godly feelings. We know that just as God loves all the people He made, so He wants *us*

We must treat all people as equals

to love all the people He made. God wants us to live this way.

Just as He forgives us if we are sorry for the wrong things we do, so God wants us to forgive other people for the wrongs they do.

If we remember that all people are equal as God's children, and if we treat them all as children of God, then we know the most important thing of all.

What we have learned so far

We must always remember that what we know is only a very small part of all knowledge. Even the wisest people on earth do not know the answers to some of the simplest mysteries. Yet that small part that we do know is the heart of all knowledge. For we know that God gave us rules by which to live, that God wants us to live with love and fairness and peace toward our fellow men.

Our own people, the Jews, throughout many years, have tried to make human rules that would help us carry out this great Godly wish of love and fairness and peace. Life is easier and happier when we understand those rules.

QUESTIONS TO THINK ABOUT

1. Can you think of any "mysteries" in nature like the fact that there are vegetables and fruits in every color except "sky-blue"?

2. We use such words as "Lord," "King," "Ruler of the World," "Heavenly Father" and others when we speak of God. Do you remember any of the Hebrew words used for God in our prayers?

QUESTIONS TO ASK YOUR PARENTS

1. Ask your parents about the migration of salmon; what we know and what we do not know about this.

2. Although there are many things we do not know about God, we know how God wants us to live. For example, how do we know that God wants us to rest on the Sabbath?

UNIT THREE

What Judaism Teaches Us About Right and Wrong

CHAPTER XI

We Can Choose Between Right and Wrong

We don't know everything about God. But we do know that God knows everything about us. And this brings us to one of the greatest puzzles of human life. For it seems that if God knows everything that is going to happen, then everything each of us does has already been decided in advance. And if everything we do is decided in advance, how can we choose between right and wrong?

Yet just as we feel in our hearts that God knows everything, so we feel in our hearts that we can choose between right and wrong. Rabbi Akiba, who lived long ago, tells us that both things are true: God knows everything that is going to happen, and yet each man must decide for himself between right and wrong.

To help us decide, God gave us rules for the right way to live. But we also have urges to break these rules. Each of us sometimes feels he has two whispers in his ears, the good whisper and the bad whisper. One tells us what is right, and the other tempts us to do what is wrong. In Hebrew this urge is called a *yetzer*.

A *yetzer* is like a wish, an advice and an urge, all in one. The good urge, or the wish to do good, is called the *yetzer ha-tov*. The wish to do wrong is called the *yetzer ha-ra*.

Some people like to make excuses for doing wrong by saying, "I couldn't help it." They say everything is decided in advance. They say, a poor boy who is born in the slums steals because he is hungry, and is bad because life is bad in the slums.

If a rich boy steals, then they say something must be the matter with him. It is psychological. Therefore he can't help what he does.

We cannot choose some things

Now, we all know that there are many things in our lives which we cannot choose. That is what makes it so easy to say that we cannot choose anything at all. First, let us see what we really cannot choose.

It is perfectly true that we cannot

choose where and to whom we are born. We cannot choose our parents, our brothers, our sisters.

We cannot choose the time and place of our birth. Indeed, we often like to daydream about being born in some other time and somewhere else in the world. Some of us dream of having been born in the time of Columbus, so we could be explorers, discover America, and meet the Indians. Then we think: but it is even more exciting to be born in our own time, when we may explore the moon.

But we know we really cannot choose about this.

We cannot choose what we look like. We cannot choose our height or the color of our eyes or skin.

We cannot choose our talents. Artis-

A 17th century boy could choose to discover gravity or invent a microscope

A 20th century boy can explore the moon or discover a cure for cancer

tic talent, as we say, is "something you either have or you haven't got." We cannot choose to be geniuses in writing or art or music. Nevertheless, we can learn to sing better, or play the piano better, or draw better. We can improve our skills, but as for talent or genius, this is inborn. We are either born with it or without it.

We cannot choose the weather. We cannot choose when we want it to snow or when we want the rain to stop falling.

But, even in the things we absolutely cannot do, there are certain changes we can make, if we want to strongly enough. We can learn to play the piano, even if we are not geniuses. We can prepare ourselves for the weather by building houses. This is because we have will power.

It is this will power that God gave us, that makes it possible for us to choose between right and wrong, between the good whisper and the bad whisper. This is called freedom of will.

You can see how you really make your own choices a hundred times a day.

What we can choose

Suppose a new child moves into your neighborhood. He stands there and watches you and your friends playing ball. Your *yetzer ha-tov,* your good impulse, tells you to call him to join the game. Your *yetzer ha-ra* whispers to you to keep him out. Maybe there is even something your *yetzer ha-ra* can find to pick on. Maybe the new child is from a different country and speaks broken English and is easy to make fun of. Or maybe he is too dressed up, or maybe he is short, or skinny, or squinty. Your *yetzer ha-ra* can find all sorts of excuses for you to be unfriendly. But you know what is right and what is wrong, and you can choose to be friendly.

Your bad whisper can get you to behave badly, not only with strangers, but even with your own friends. This can happen even in the smallest things. You are walking home from school with two friends. You have a package of chewing-gum, and you take some for yourself. You feel you ought to share it around, but you also would like to keep it all for yourself. Of course you do have the freedom of will to tell yourself, "I don't want to be a selfish person," and to pass around the gum.

The next step in selfishness can be more dangerous. Suppose one of your friends pulls a handkerchief out of his pocket, and you see a dime roll out. You know it is wrong to pick up the dime and keep it. You know you ought to tell your friend he dropped his money. In such things, the *yetzer ha-ra* is very easy to recognize. It can't fool you about whether it is right or wrong to take other people's money.

But sometimes, even though you know what is right, the *yetzer ha-ra* can fool you by telling you it doesn't

Sometimes the *yetzer ha-ra* fools you by telling you it doesn't matter

matter. You are taking something from the refrigerator and a glass falls and breaks. Nobody is in the kitchen to notice. You sweep the pieces away. Maybe mother will never miss the glass. If she does, she may think someone else broke it. But you know it would be right to tell her about it, even if she will never find out.

It isn't always easy to choose

Of course in such cases it is easy to know what is right and what is wrong, just as in the movies or TV it is usually easy to know who are the good guys and who are the bad guys. But in life things are not always so simple. There are times when things do seem to "gang up" on us to make even good intentions turn bad.

Suppose it is your birthday. You open the gifts—and there are three sweaters. Along comes Aunt Esther with her birthday present. You unwrap it and find a fourth sweater! Aunt Esther says she hopes you like it. Should you lie and say that it is just what you wanted? It isn't easy to think of the right thing at the right time, but you could say, "It's a beautiful sweater. But look, Aunt Esther, I got three other sweaters for my birthday. Would it be too much trouble to exchange it for something else?"

As we grow wiser, we know there are always ways to keep from lying or from hurting people's feelings and to do what is right. We have minds of our own to think of these ways. And we have the power to hold back our bad urges and to choose to do the right thing. This is called freedom of will.

What we have learned so far

Because we have freedom of will, no person can say, "I can't help being bad." No person is forced by being born in the slums, or by being born too rich, to become Public Enemy Number One. No person has to be a public enemy at all. No person has to be a gangster, or a juvenile delinquent.

It is true that some people are "born on the wrong side of the tracks" and some people don't have the good fortune of a good home and loving parents. But all of us do have a will power, a freedom of will, to choose between right and wrong, between the good whisper and the bad whisper.

QUESTIONS TO THINK ABOUT

1. We are told in this chapter there are many things in our life which we cannot choose—such as our parents. Can you name five other things about ourselves that we cannot choose?

2. Do you remember a time when you found it hard to decide between a wrong choice and a right choice—and why you finally made the right choice?

QUESTIONS TO ASK YOUR PARENTS

1. Explain to your parents the "yetzer ha-tov" and the "yetzer ha-ra." How does this help to explain why we sometimes find it hard to decide what to do?

2. We are told that one of the greatest puzzles in human life is the idea that God knows everything that is going to happen, yet we feel that each man must decide for himself what is right and what is wrong. Ask your parents how they think this is possible.

CHAPTER XII

Why Should We Choose What Is Right?

We now know that we are free to choose between the good urge and the bad urge, between the *yetzer ha-tov* and the *yetzer ha-ra*. Why should we always choose what is good and what is right? Why not choose to do wrong?

The easiest answer is that we choose good because we will be punished if we do wrong. In fact, that is the way we teach animals! If the animal does what we want, it gets a reward—we give the animal something it likes to eat. If the animal behaves badly, we punish it. We keep away its food.

If a dog is good, we pat it and give it a biscuit. We slap it when it snaps at a friend.

That is also how we teach very young children who are too young to understand. We try to teach them to be good by rewards. And when they are naughty, we sometimes punish them by not giving them the things they want, like ice cream, or candy. We may even spank them.

We are afraid to do wrong

Long ago, when people first began to think about laws of right and wrong, they decided that the simplest thing was to punish people for doing wrong. That is still done today. When a thief is caught, he is usually sent to prison. When we drive recklessly, and put other people in danger by going through a red light, we are punished—we have to pay a fine. And sometimes we even lose our permit to drive.

But much of the time when we choose between good and bad, right and wrong, there is no one to see what we do; there is no one to reward or punish us.

If no one sees what we do, why should we choose the good? Is it only for reward that we do good?

Some people believe that if they do good they will be rewarded in heaven. They "save up good deeds" for the world to come.

But this is not the real reason either, for choosing good instead of bad.

You do right, not for praise, but because you know it *is* right

Doing good makes us feel good

We choose to do good because it makes us feel good, feel clean inside, just as a bath makes us feel nice and clean outside.

Suppose you are walking home from school. You see a little child with some candy in his hand. You would never dream of taking candy from a little kid! Even though you are bigger and stronger and could easily do it, the taste of the candy would never be sweet enough to make up for the mean feeling you would have at doing such a thing.

In such a simple case, you do what is right because of your feeling about it. You would feel disgusted with yourself if you did anything else.

You don't do what is right because you believe this will help you go to heaven. You do it simply because you *know* what is right. And this makes you a tiny little bit like God, who knows all that is right and wrong. You even feel closer to God.

The Bible tells us, right at the beginning in the story of Adam and Eve, that it was this very knowledge, the knowledge of what was good and what was evil, that made people like God.

When the serpent came to Eve in the Garden of Eden and tried to tempt her to eat the forbidden fruit, Eve told the serpent she was afraid she would die if she tasted it. But the serpent said, "You won't die." He told her, "God knows that on the day you eat the fruit of this tree your eyes shall be opened and you shall be like God, knowing good and evil."

And then, after Eve coaxed Adam to taste the fruit of the tree, the Bible tells us, "The Lord God said, 'Behold, the man is become as one of us, to know good and evil.'"

And then, God sent Adam and Eve out into the world, where they would have to work and be with others and have every kind of pain and joy, having to choose between right and wrong. Wasn't this like what happens to each baby as it grows up into life?

At first it is protected and given everything it needs. But as it grows up it must learn the difference between right and wrong, and it must test all this in the world. And as each baby grows into a child and each child into a man or woman, it has to decide for itself more and more, what is right and what is wrong. And so each person growing up, can become a little more like God.

Each of us sometimes makes a bargain with himself, imagining it is a bargain with God. You may say to yourself, "I want a new bicycle for my birthday, and I am going to be very good! I am going to stop teasing my little sister from now until my birthday. Then God will reward me with the bicycle."

Yet something else inside you tells you that you cannot make a bargain with God, you can't trade being good or being bad for a bicycle.

Because the difference between good and bad is already far more precious than bicycles and vacations and anything on earth. It is already the thing that makes us less like animals, and a little more like God.

Animals don't know the difference between right and wrong, unless we tell them. A big dog will grab the food away from a little dog. We can't blame the animal, because it can't tell the difference between right and wrong. It can only tell the difference between punishment and reward.

But people can choose between

good and bad, even without reward or punishment. We have a little bit of God in us, that helps us know the difference. This is what sets us apart from animals.

Doing good helps us to be holy

There is another way in which we can see the wonderful system that brings human beings further and further away from the animals, and helps us come closer and closer to understanding the beautiful plan of God's universe. The second great difference between human beings and animals is that we can not only know good from bad, but we can pass on our knowledge to our children. In this way, as the world grows older, people know more and more about what is good and what is bad.

Jews have been learning about right and wrong for a very long time. For instance, many of the stories of our early Rabbis show us that they still believed in punishment and reward as the reason for choosing what is right. They believed in the reward in the world to come, if not in this world.

Yet at the same time, they had already been told the higher truth, that to do what is right is to be holy, to be like God.

We all know that children can be told important things which they do not understand until much later. A whole people, too, can be in its childhood. The Jewish people was still quite young when Moses brought them the word of God, and it took the people many centuries to understand it. We are not yet finished growing and understanding. The Bible tells us, "And the Lord spoke unto Moses, saying, 'Speak unto all the congregation of the children of Israel, and say unto them: Ye shall be holy, for I the Lord your God am holy.'" And then Moses told the people God's rules of right and wrong.

There, from the time of Moses, we see that by doing right we become more like God, who is holy.

Doing good helps improve the world

God also gave us the gift of adding to our knowledge, from father to son.

From one generation to the next, people learn to make life easier, and more healthful. In the same way, we add to our laws and to our moral knowledge.

We are able to think and to speak and to write, so we can pass on our knowledge and make the world we live in better and better. When the wheel was first invented, it made life much easier. It made it possible for men to move things, to build without carrying everything on their own backs or the backs of animals.

With the wheel, we made wagons and then automobiles and trains. We developed the cog-wheel that turns so much machinery from clocks to dynamos.

In the same way, we have learned to make writing easier and easier. First men scratched the messages on stones, or in clay. Then they learned to write on paper. Then the printing press was invented. Each step made it possible to pass on more and more knowledge to more and more people.

People wanted to stop pain and suffering, so they learned more and more about medicine, until it became the wonderful science that it is today.

And people have always studied the rules of right and wrong. They came far away from the early ideas of making bargains with God, just as modern doctors came far away from the early magic of medicine-men.

Our Jewish prophets and rabbis have always tried to bring us closer and closer to what Judaism calls the "Kingdom of God." The Kingdom of God is the time in the future when mankind will have learned to be more like God, and to turn away from the *yetzer ha-ra.*

Two stories about right and wrong

Here are two little stories that show the difference between the early way of understanding our reason for doing right, and the way we understand it now.

The first story is about a very poor Jew in the ancient city of Babylon. One day he was looking for work in the market place, so that he might buy food for his family. A man hired him to carry five heavy pots to a mansion. The pay for his work was usually a copper coin for each pot, but when the job was finished the poor Jew was given only three coppers. He then asked for five, but the rich man insulted him, called him a stupid clod, and chased him away.

The poor Jew gave the three coins to his wife, who ran to buy food. And then she saw that one of the coins was not copper, but gold. She took it home to her husband. Even though he had been insulted and underpaid, the poor Jew hurried to the rich man's house, told the owner he had made a mistake, and gave back the golden coin.

But the rich man was the prophet Elijah in disguise! And instead of taking back the golden coin, he made all three coins turn into gold. And each time the poor man spent one of the gold coins and was given copper in his change, the copper coins turned into more gold!

Such a tale tells us that honesty will be rewarded with real gold.

Now, here is a story for today: Suppose you find a wallet on the street. You look inside and find three dollar bills, a name and a telephone number. You take the wallet home and telephone the owner to tell him you have found his wallet, and where to come for it. When he comes and thanks you for it, don't you feel good all over? Don't you feel really grown up? Can't you almost hear the whisper of your *yetzer ha-tov*, inside of you, saying, "I'm proud of you!" Only it is more like singing, instead of just whispering. You feel a little more like God.

That is what the old story meant; that is what we mean by a truly golden reward.

What we have learned so far

Judaism believes that man has been given freedom of will so that he may take part in learning for himself what is right and what is wrong, of discovering for himself what God wants. Then, when we do what is right, we are in harmony with God's laws, and our own free will is in harmony with God's will. This gives us a happiness that is different from any other. Even the smallest child has known a touch of this happiness.

QUESTIONS TO THINK ABOUT

1. Is a person good because he fears punishment if he is bad?
2. Did you ever feel good because you did something good without fear of punishment or hope of reward? Describe what happened.

QUESTIONS TO ASK YOUR PARENTS

1. Life in the Garden of Eden is sometimes compared to the life of a baby because everything is done by the parents to make the baby comfortable. When the child begins to leave his parents, he must decide for himself between good and evil and he must then "eat the fruit of the tree of knowledge." What do your parents think of this comparison?
2. One generation of Jews passes on its ideas of right and wrong to the next generation. Ask your parents to describe how they are doing this for you.

UNIT FOUR

What Judaism Teaches Us About the Right Way

CHAPTER XIII

Justice Is the Right Way

If each man is able to tell right from wrong, why do we have laws and policemen and courts? Judaism tells us that each man has a little bit of God in him that shows him right from wrong. And yet, for thousands of years we Jews have been trying very hard to make rules that will help men do what is right and avoid what is wrong.

Of course, often we know what is right and yet we don't do it. Our evil urge, our selfishness, or even our animal wishes, may keep us from being as good as we know how.

The simplest way to do right is by what every child and every grownup calls "playing fair." Even the smallest child, when he first learns how to play hide and seek, knows that it isn't fair to peek.

Fairness is what we learn as soon as we begin to deal with other people. As soon as we begin to know the people around us, we have to take their rights into account. Sometimes what they want is not what we want. There have to be rules to help us decide between the wants of different people. These rules of fairness we call "justice."

Each person has rights

Justice is a way of deciding what is most fair.

When two automobiles bump into each other, what seems fair to one driver hardly ever seems fair to the other. And quite often it is true that each one is a little bit to blame.

In our Jewish idea of justice, we begin with the idea that each person has his rights. This was not always so in ancient times. And in many parts of the world it is not even so today.

In ancient times, a king was always right. But in the Jewish idea of justice, this changed. The prophet Nathan could stand before King David and accuse him of taking away another man's wife, just as plainly as if King David were an ordinary citizen.

There are still some countries, in modern times, where dictators rule in much the same way that kings used to rule. Modern dictators, like the kings of old, can execute a man, without a trial, just because they want to.

But the Jews knew this was wrong from the very beginning of their religion. In the Ten Commandments, it was put down that each person had a right to his life. The sixth Commandment tells us, "Thou shalt not commit murder."

This Commandment was brought to the Jewish people by Moses. But they also learned this rule from the story of Cain and Abel which went way back to the beginning of knowledge. It told them plainly that when Cain killed his brother, he had the mark of the murderer put upon him and was driven into exile.

We also know that each person has a right to his property: stealing is wrong. The eighth Commandment tells us, "Thou shalt not steal."

Justice is based on truth

If there is going to be justice, then we must be able to know the facts of each case. Therefore, people must tell the truth. And so the very next Commandment, the ninth, tells us, "Thou shalt not bear false witness."

In ancient times a king was always right

But Nathan could stand before King David and accuse him

Now, here is one of the favorite points where the *yetzer ha-ra* attacks us. Whenever we have an argument, our bad urge is likely to suggest a way by which we can get around telling the real truth and yet seem to be telling the truth. Our rabbis tell a story about this kind of trick:

A man named Bartholomew was given a hundred coins for safekeeping. One day his friend asked for the money back, and Bartholomew said, "Why, I put it back in your hand!"

His friend said Bartholomew was lying. "Meet me in the synagogue," cried Bartholomew, "and I will swear it!" Then Bartholomew went home, took a hollow reed, and put the coins inside. Using the reed for a cane, he went to the synagogue to meet his friend.

When they stood before the rabbi, Bartholomew gave his friend the stick and said, "Just hold this in your hand for me while I swear." And then he raised his right arm and swore, "By the Lord of this sacred synagogue, I swear that the money you put into my hand in trust, I have given back into your hand."

But just then, his friend, who hadn't realized how heavy the stick was, dropped it. The coins rolled out!

To this day, we have a saying, "The truth will always come out!" There must be no tricks with truth, for without truth it is impossible to have justice.

Justice does not always mean there is an argument that has to be decided by a rabbi or a judge or an umpire. It is a way of behaving in every moment of our lives. For we want each person around us to get the fairest share out of life.

It is fair to share work and fun

In our family, for instance, it is fair for everyone to share the work. Father works to earn money that buys the food and clothing and books and other things we need. Mother works to prepare our meals, to keep the house in order. It is only fair for the children to do a little work, to pick up their own clothes and toys, and keep their things in order, and to run errands.

With our friends, it is only fair to take turns in everything. In some groups the same child wants to be the leader all the time, but others have a right to their turn to lead, too.

Neighbors and strangers have certain rights

With our neighbors, it is only fair to respect their property, not to make too much noise when they want to rest, and not to break their bushes or let the Sunday papers blow onto their lawn.

Even with strangers, we must always think of what is fair. If we are in a movie, and want to say something about the picture, it is only fair to keep our voice low, so as not to spoil the movie for others all around us.

You can often see grownups being thoughtful of other people's rights, in little things they do. When father parks his car, he is careful not to park too close to the man ahead of him, so the other man will have room to get out. He doesn't know the other man, but he is thinking of him.

We must be fair to ourselves too

It is not only to our family, our neighbors, our friends, and all the people around us that we want to be fair. We must be fair to ourselves.

If someone hits you for no reason at all, it is only fair for you to defend yourself. You are not fair to yourself if you just let him beat you up, without even trying to protect yourself. Some people say, if you are hit on one cheek, turn the other. But Judaism does not believe this is fair, or that people will learn justice in this way.

Our great teacher, Hillel, long ago said, "If I am not for myself, who will be for me?" Each of us must have self-respect, or he will not be able to respect others. But just as importantly, Hillel went on to say, "If I am *only* for myself, what am I?"

Laws tell us what is fair

To help us be fair to ourselves and all others, there are customs and rules. These reach out and change, as our lives change.

In a game, whether it is baseball or jump-rope, there are rules to tell what

How law developed

1. Killing for the loss of a tooth

is fair. When a new game is invented, the rules are invented, too. When the way of playing changes, the rules are changed. Everyone is very careful to be fair.

In the same way, people have rules and laws for fairness in living. They have neighborhood laws, and city laws, and state laws, and even federal laws, like here in the United States. And now, we are building up a set of world laws. These laws are like a nest of boxes fitting inside each other, for the heart of all the laws is in the Ten Commandments.

Judaism brought new ideas of justice

Before the Ten Commandments and the laws of the Torah were given to the Jews, people did not think very much about justice. Sometimes they took a very big revenge for a very small crime, because they had not thought out how to be fair.

Suppose you took some marbles

2. A footh for a tooth

3. The value of a tooth for the loss of a tooth ... law begins to grow

4. The law grows and grows ... and civilized nations use judges and courts to settle disputes

from a boy, and he got even by coming and taking your bicycle! You would certainly cry out that this was unfair, though of course you shouldn't have taken his marbles in the first place.

In the olden days, if a man knocked out another man's tooth, the second man might come back and kill the first man. So the old Jewish law said, "A tooth for a tooth," and not a life for a tooth! Soon the rabbis explained that the Torah did not mean another tooth—but only the value of the tooth, in return for such an injury. The value of a tooth might be different to a movie star than to a boxer. That, too, had to be thought out. And so the law grew, and grew, and grew, as each case was judged, to show what should be fair. And that is the basic idea of the law all over the civilized world today.

Judges and courts

To decide each case, we have to have judges. We can read in the Bible how Moses began to judge the people, after he brought them the Torah from Mount Sinai. Everyone came to him, with every quarrel, and he sat "from morning to night." His father-in-law said this would wear Moses out. "Hearken now unto my voice," he advised, "thou shalt provide out of all the people able men, such as God-fearing men, men of truth ... and they

89

shall judge the people at all seasons. And let it be that every great matter they shall bring to thee, and every small matter they shall judge themselves..."

So even today we have a system of courts, from the small claims court to the supreme court, just as was started by Moses.

After what is fair has been decided, we have police officers and a whole system of law, to make sure that justice is carried out.

This has always been the way of Judaism. "Justice, justice shalt thou follow," is written in the Torah. And the prophet Micah, too, reminded us that we know what is right, and we should only do justice. Micah said, "It hath been told thee, O man, what is good, and what the Lord doth require of thee." And what does the Lord require? "Only to do justly, and to love mercy, and to walk humbly with thy God."

What we have learned so far

Justice is the way of making sure that what is right is done. Every person has certain rights, and God wants us to live and to do the best we can with our lives.

We must therefore be fair to ourselves, and to all other people, even the people we don't know. That is why we have laws and officers and judges to help us be fair.

QUESTIONS TO THINK ABOUT

1. The best way to understand "justice" is to think of "playing fair." Can you think of a time when you told a friend that he wasn't playing fair? What did he say?
2. Which of the commandments tells us what we must not do in order to be just to our neighbors?

QUESTIONS TO ASK YOUR PARENTS

1. Being fair and just with our family means sharing the work in the home. What do your parents think that your share should be?
2. Judges and courts help us to find justice. Can your parents help you find a story in a newspaper about a court which decided a case justly?

CHAPTER XIV

Charity, Mercy and Love Are the Right Ways

From far back, Judaism teaches us to be fair and to have laws so that each person will receive an equal chance for fair treatment. And yet as we see the world, it sometimes does not seem fair at all. There are rich people who have too much of everything, and poor people who don't even have enough to eat.

There are countries in the world where people have little to eat, no hospitals, and only huts to live in.

Does this seem fair?

In the beginning, as the Bible tells us, there was chaos. And slowly, slowly, in a great and beautiful plan that we cannot yet understand, that chaos is being turned into a world of order and knowledge. Slowly, slowly, men are learning how to live better lives and how to be fair to each other.

And slowly they are learning how to control the wild forces of nature, so that there will be food for all and schools and good things in life for everyone. In Judaism we say that "in the end of days," we will have filled out the plan of God, so there will be peace and plenty for all.

But while we are still finding the way out of chaos, there is much that is unequal in the world, that cannot be helped by judges and by laws.

Charity is a way of helping others

On the opposite side, to help people against misfortune, there is charity. It is a kind of justice. Our ancestors understood this so well that they used the same word for justice and for charity. The Hebrew word for "righteousness" is "tzedek," and the Hebrew word for charity is "tzedakah," or making things right.

Charity is a special kind of justice. It is a way of being fair when there is no one to blame for the unfairness. And in Judaism, this is a duty. We must share what we have with those who don't have.

The Rabbis thought that charity was so important that they told many stories about it. One of them was about Elijah and a wealthy man who owned much land. He lost everything, until only a tiny field remained on which he could hardly make a living for himself and his wife. Yet when he was asked for charity, he said to his wife, "Let us sell half the field, so we can help the poor." She agreed, and when Elijah saw what they had done, he placed a treasure in the remaining half that they still owned. So a good man was rewarded, because even when he lost his riches, he wanted to share what he had left.

For in the old days as today, not everyone knew how to be charitable. We have a saying from Samaria, where there were many kinds of nut trees. Rabbi Bar Levi said, "There are three kinds of nuts, the soft-shelled that open by themselves, and the second kind that open if you tap them, and the third kind that you can beat on a stone and still they won't open! So it is with people," he said, "Some open their purse without being asked, some need first to be tapped, and others are harder than stone." Don't we still say, today, "So-and-so is a hard nut to crack."

The best ways of giving

But just as there were always hard nuts to crack, there were people who not only taught us to be charitable, but who worried about the best ways of giving charity. To give is good, but if we share with people who don't know where the gift comes from, that is even better.

Why? It is better for ourselves, so that we don't give charity in order to be thanked for it. And it is better for the person receiving it, so that he may not feel embarrassed. Our Rabbis had a saying, "It is better for a man to throw himself into a fiery furnace, rather than to put his neighbor to shame."

Today it is easier for us to give help without knowing exactly to whom it goes, for we have great charity organizations to collect and give out the money. But already in the Temple, in Jerusalem, there was a secret corner where donors could leave their gifts unseen, and people could secretly come and be helped.

Maimonides, the great Jewish thinker in the Middle Ages, put down the rules of charity. The best kind of charity, he said, is to share in such a way as to help people reach the point where they can take care of themselves.

We do this today for our pioneers who are building anew the country of Israel. By giving money to the United Jewish Appeal or other such charitable organizations, we are helping Israel to build factories and to start new farm settlements, so that poor refugees who come to Israel may soon be able to earn a living.

Many people—not only Jews—now understand that such charity is a way of hastening the day when people all over the world will have a fairer life. So charity is not only given by each person now, but by whole nations. The United States has a vast program of giving away money and sending experts to backward countries to show those people how to better their lives. We show them how to make their soil fertile, how to grow the right crops, how to make and use modern tools.

We also have schools to teach handicapped people work that they can do. Everyone feels better at being able to earn his own living, and not to reach out for a gift, no matter how graciously it is given.

Many times it is preferable to give in such a way that the person receiving it does not know the name of the giver. Sometimes, however, a warm personal contact between the giver and the one he has helped is as important as the gift itself. Thus, many people pick out poor children, in their own country or in foreign lands, and help them to get an education. Both the child and the giver enjoy keeping in touch with each other.

Mercy

All this is part of the Jewish idea of "tzedakah," of justice by giving. And there is still a greater idea of giving. and this is the idea of giving help even to our enemies. It is called mercy. We know that in the old days, after a war the winning nation would try to destroy the losing nation, just as the Romans ruined Judea and carried the Jews away to become slaves. But as we grow to understand the Godliness in us, we have become less revengeful. We want to help the whole world to get over the feeling of hatred. And so today, our nation when it won a war did not punish the loser. Instead, it helped the countries to get back to normal life.

After the last war, the Allies helped the losing nations to build up their cities and their factories. The victors treated the losers with mercy.

In our own lives we sometimes show this feeling even to people who don't seem to deserve it. Suppose you are riding your bicycle. A bigger boy comes along on his bicycle and tries to cut in on you. Instead, he loses his balance and falls off his bike. He has a pocketful of marbles, and now they roll all over the sidewalk.

Because he bullied you, he has less right than usual to your sympathy. Still, you help him to get up, and to collect his marbles. You are treating him with mercy.

Why do you do this?

Because mercy is really part of our nature, a part of that little bit of God in us. God is merciful and loving to us all, and it is natural for us to feel lovingkindness, instead of feeling "tough" and telling ourselves we don't care about anybody.

Kindness is part of our nature

Kindness goes with the wish we all feel to be friendly and helpful. We all feel this most strongly toward helpless creatures. When you find a bird that has hurt its leg and is lying in your backyard, you want to help it, to feed it and give it water, even to try to put a splint on its leg, or to call the Humane Society.

Kindness and sympathy are not meant only for the poor. It is an attitude toward life. When you see a woman with her arms full of packages trying to open the door of her car, it is simply a kindness to open the door for her.

With kindness there is also thoughtfulness. A child you know has been out of school for a week. It is thoughtful and kind to offer to help her catch up with the lessons she has missed.

It is thoughtful to avoid hurting someone's feelings. Suppose you had a wonderful time at a birthday party given by one of your schoolmates. It is thoughtful not to talk about the party to the children in your class who were not invited.

It is kind and thoughtful to keep from judging other people. Things that people do may look bad or wrong to you. But until you know all about them and their reasons, it is unkind to judge them.

You already know how wise Hillel was. It was he who said, "Do not judge another person until you are in his place."

Suppose a new boy comes to school. He doesn't know the answers to the simplest questions, and you decide to call him a dunce. But then you find out that he has had a bad sickness that kept him in bed several months, and he is simply behind and trying to catch up.

Our Rabbis taught us not to go by appearances, but rather to be charitable before judging anyone. They told the story of the man who sent

We should not judge by appearances . . . the boy we think a dunce may have fallen behind in schoolwork because of illness

his son to a neighbor to borrow a measure of wheat. The boy found the neighbor in his barn, measuring wheat. But when the boy asked for some, the neighbor said, "I don't have any wheat."

The boy went home and told this to his father. "Perhaps that was wheat he has to turn over for his taxes," the father said. "Go and ask him to lend us five *shekels*." The boy went, and found the neighbor in his house, counting money. But the neighbor said, "I don't have a *shekel* to my name."

When the boy told his father this, the father said, "Perhaps it was money that he held in trust for someone."

Later the two men met. The neighbor said, "When your son found me measuring wheat and I gave him none, what did you think of me?"

"I thought it was wheat for your taxes," the father said.

"And when I gave him no money?"

"Perhaps it was trust money," the father said.

"You are a good man," his neighbor said, "for you have judged your neighbor not by appearance, but waited to know the truth." As it happened, the boy's father soon learned that both things were true.

What we have learned so far

Simply knowing that people around us view us with kindness makes us feel good. Helping others makes us feel good. Being thoughtful and kind makes us feel good. People are all in the world together, and they owe kindness to each other, simply because they all are children of God.

Charity and mercy and love are all part of the same feeling. Just as God shares creation with us with kindness and mercy and love, so we share with all other people.

QUESTIONS TO THINK ABOUT

1. People who give money to charity are compared in this chapter to three kinds of nuts. How could you use this story to get more pupils to contribute to your class collection?

2. Do you remember any time when you forgave someone who hurt you instead of trying to get revenge? Do you know why you did this?

QUESTIONS TO ASK YOUR PARENTS

1. Explain to your parents why we prefer to use the Hebrew word "tzedakah" which means "justice" instead of the word "charity." Why is *tzedakah* part of God's "plan"?

2. When we are told that we should forgive our enemies, does this mean that we should also forgive the Germans for the killing of six million Jews during World War II? Ask your parents how they feel about this.

CHAPTER XV

Brotherhood Is the Right Way

Judaism teaches us that all men are brothers. Just as the brothers and sisters in every family love each other and feel that they must always help each other, so every human being should have this feeling for every other human being.

When God created the first man, we are told, He took dust from all four corners of the world. He took the red earth and black earth and white, and He made Adam. Why did He make only one man? So that all the people of the earth would have the same ancestor and would be equal. Then no one would be able to say that he came from better stock than did his neighbor.

Yet people do say this, and even brothers quarrel. For we see that God allowed the evil urge to exist too, in order that man should struggle against evil, and find out what is good and what is bad. God made sure that the feeling for brotherhood in us is strong enough to overcome these bad feelings.

One of our Bible stories tells us about all these feelings in a single family. The feeling of brotherhood struggles against the feelings of envy and jealousy. And in the end, justice, mercy and human kindness come together in brotherly love.

This is the story of Joseph and his brothers. Joseph was a bright young boy, and became his father's favorite son. And his father Jacob gave him a handsome coat of many colors. Joseph was a bit of a show-off, and he paraded the coat before his brothers who were working in the field. They became envious, seized him, and sold him to some traders who were passing with a caravan. Joseph was taken to Egypt where he grew up and later on became the Prime Minister. There was famine everywhere, but Joseph had been wise and stored a great deal of food. Because of the famine, his brothers came to Egypt in order to buy food, and they came to Joseph without knowing who he was. But he knew who they were. He recognized them. And instead of being hateful and taking vengeance, he was deeply moved and helped them; and in the end the family was reunited.

This story of Joseph tells us something very important. It is not only a story of a Jewish family, but of the whole "family of nations" of the whole world. It means that human brotherhood holds us together, even when some people have been mean. It means that we should always help each other, with charity, with mercy, and with brotherly love.

People are alike but different

In the old times, when travel was slow and people could travel only by horse, or camel, or on sailing boats, they were more likely to be afraid of strangers. A person of a different color, even of different dress, was feared. Today it is not only easier for us to reach and know one another, but today our sciences have shown us how alike we are to each other. Today we know that all living beings develop in the same way, from cells, yet they still may be different.

There are about three billion peo-

Joseph was not vengeful toward his family, but showed them mercy

ple in the world. Do you think there is a single one who looks, acts, sounds, or thinks exactly like you? Even twins who look alike are not exactly identical. Each person is different from all the other people in the world.

In the wondrous variety of God's world there are myriads of different creatures. Among dogs alone there are poodles, and dachshunds, and sheepdogs, and terriers, and collies. There are thousands of different plants, from the blade of grass to the spreading oak tree.

And so among people, there are white and brown and black; there are pygmies and there are seven feet tall basketball players. They have different likes and dislikes. One child likes books, another likes bowling.

People have different customs. In our part of the world we say "ladies first." But in some other parts of the world it is the custom for the woman to walk behind the man.

In our part of the world women wear dresses and trousers, just as they like, but in other countries they may never wear trousers. And in still other countries the women wear trousers and the men wear robes.

And as it is with the way they dress, people have different ideas about God. Different religions tell them different ways in which to serve God.

When travel was slow and difficult, people had strange ideas about those in far places of the world who had a different color, or a different cast of features. Now we know that such differences do not matter. They do not make people better, or worse, or brighter, or stronger.

We know that neither the kind of eyes or nose, nor the color of skin, makes anyone more beautiful. There is beauty in every kind and in every color.

Differences make life better

These differences make life more interesting. That is why we say, "Variety is the spice of life." It wouldn't be very interesting if all food tasted the same, and if all candy were peppermint.

If all people had the same talents, we might have only musicians and no scientists, or only schoolteachers and nobody to bake cookies. If all people thought alike, Columbus would never have set out to prove the world was round. And he would never have discovered America.

We see that opposite things are put together to make a good world. People are different, and yet they are alike, and that is what makes life so interesting. People may not always live equally on earth, but we are all equal before God. He made us all and loves us all—the rich and poor, the weak and strong, the colored and white, the pretty and not-so-pretty, the Jew and the non-Jew.

King Christian of Denmark wore the same armband as the Jews

Brotherhood is fair play

Belief in God makes us believe in the brotherhood of mankind. If we are fair, we accept and respect people as God made them.

Suppose your school is having an exhibition of Thanksgiving drawings. Each pupil is asked to vote for the best drawing in his class, to be sent to the big exhibition. When a drawing is shown, you don't know and you don't care whether the child who made it is white or colored, Jew or Christian, rich or poor. You just vote for the best drawing.

It is as easy to be fair to a person as to a drawing. If we treat people with fairness and kindness, no matter how different they are from us, we are treating them like children of God, in brotherhood.

Suppose a new girl joins your class. She has just come from Italy and she knows very little English. You are being fair if you realize it is just as odd for you not to know Italian as for her not to know English. If you then try to understand and help her, you are being kind. You have added love to justice.

We had a wonderful example of justice and lovingkindness during the terrible days of the Nazis in Europe. The Nazis sent away the Jews from each country and tried to kill them all. When the Nazis came to Denmark, they ordered the Jews to wear yellow armbands. In that way it was

101

easier for the Nazis to find all the Jews.

But the king of Denmark, King Christian, spoiled the plan. He, too, put on a yellow armband, and the Danish Christians then did the same. So many Christians were wearing yellow armbands that the Nazis could not tell which of the people were Jews.

What the king and his people did was an act of love and brotherhood.

What we have learned so far

Though people are different in many ways, we are all equally children of God. In Israel, for example, we can see how different colors and different eyes do not make people very different—because Jews who have lived in all the different countries of the world have come back to their homeland. There we see black Jews and brown Jews and white Jews, Jews with slant-eyes and Jews with straight eyes, but we know they are all brothers.

So it should be all over the world, because *all* people are brothers. When we feel the brotherhood of people, we give more freedom to the lovingkindness in us, and we understand the equality of justice. This is really the best way of showing our love of God.

QUESTIONS TO THINK ABOUT

1. There are many legends told about the creation of Adam to prove that all men are brothers. Do you remember the legend told in this chapter? Could you make up a legend of your own to prove the same idea?

2. How many differences can you find among the pupils in your own class? Would you enjoy being in the class if the pupils were more alike or less alike? Why?

QUESTIONS TO ASK YOUR PARENTS

1. The story of Joseph ends with Joseph forgiving his brothers for selling him into slavery and tells how he helps his family to be reunited. Ask your parents what this story tells us about brothers in Bible times.

2. We are told that all Jews in Israel who consider themselves as brothers are different in color, some being black, some brown and some white. Ask your parents what this should mean to us in our ideas of the brotherhood of all peoples.

CHAPTER XVI

Self-Respect and Humility Are the Right Ways

You may often wonder at the way people give you opposite answers about things. In the last chapter you had to keep in mind that all people are different from each other, but also, that all people are the same. This is only an easy example of how opposite ideas are often true.

It is like the puzzle that people in the time of Columbus couldn't understand. If one ship sailed east and the other sailed west, Columbus told them, the ships would meet! They thought he was crazy. But today every child knows this seemingly odd thing is true, because the world is round, and the ships were really sailing in a circle.

Here is another contradiction. To make a pole stand up, you have to pull it downward. Everyone has seen a pole with guy-ropes all round it. One end of each rope is tied to the top of the pole; the other end is fastened to a peg in the ground. The ropes on opposite sides of the pole are pulling against each other, to hold the pole straight up.

So it is with thinking. Thinking in opposite ways helps us to keep our balance in life. It is how we balance our characters.

Sometimes we think we are terribly important. Sometimes we think we don't count at all. Judaism teaches us the healthy balance between these two feelings. It teaches us first that we must know the wonder of man, for this gives each man self-respect. But we must also know the smallness of man in the universe. This gives us humility.

Every child has found this out in his own home. You hear your parents saying that "the children come first." So you feel very important. And then, you are on the telephone and Mother suddenly tells you to hang up because she has to make a call and "who do you think you are!"

You already know that both things are true. You really are the most im-

In winter many birds must fly to warmer climates

portant thing in the world to your parents, and at times you really are just a pipsqueak.

And so with mankind. Man is the "crown of creation." Man is the most wonderful being of all that is in the universe. And at the same time he is only a speck in the universe, a tiny flicker that burns for a short time and goes out.

If we keep these two truths balanced in our minds and souls, we will know how to live, both for ourselves and for other people.

Man is the "crown of creation"

Judaism reminds us that man is the "crown of creation." The Bible describes the place of man in the universe by saying man is made in the image of God. We know this does not actually mean God has a body and our bodies are like His body. It simply means that our spirit is a tiny spark of God.

Man is "but little lower than the angels," the Bible tells us, but higher than all other creatures because he knows right and wrong. To know what is right and to do it, is a crown of glory and honor.

We can easily see the ways in which man has been gifted. Man is not limited by the natural limits of his body. Man can learn to go beyond those limits.

In the cold of winter, a bird flies south to keep warm. But human beings have found out how to make clothes, like added skins around their bodies, so they are not limited by this fact of nature.

Animals must find food where it grows. But we are not limited in that way. We have learned how to plant seeds and make food grow where we want it.

This is how God made man. The Rabbis told us that God created only the first man, so that all who came afterward should know they are brothers. But the Rabbis give us still another reason why God made only one man. "Only one single man was created in the world, to teach that if any man causes a single soul to perish, it is as though he had caused the whole world to perish." For the wonder of one man is like the wonder of the whole world.

We respect ourselves and all other people

Because of this great wonder that is man, our religion has taught us that each of us must have a great respect for his own person. Each of us must respect his body and keep it healthy and clean. Each of us must respect his mind and keep it healthy and alert.

A story is told about Hillel, a rabbi of long ago, and this simple duty. His pupils loved so much to study with him, that they would hardly let him go for a single moment. Once, when he got up to leave their circle, they asked, "Rabbi, where are you going?"

"To do a pious deed," he said with a twinkle.

"What may that be?" they asked.

And Hillel said, "To take a bath!"

"But is that a pious deed?"

"Yes," he said, "for if the Greeks, who live among us, give a man the task of washing and tending the statues of kings, which they have set up in the theaters and circuses, and if they give him food and lodging and even honors for doing so, how much more is it obligatory for me to polish and wash my body, since I have been created in the image of God!"

As we respect the wonders of our own body and mind, so we respect the wonderful creation that is each other person in the world. Each has a spark of God in him. Each is as important as all creation.

We honor our parents

Whether we know that person, or whether he is a perfect stranger, whether he is the same color as we are or not, he is a wondrous creation, a human being, and is owed the same respect we have for ourselves.

In addition to respect there is honor. The fifth Commandment tells us: "Honor thy father and thy mother." When we honor our parents, we listen to them and respect what they tell us. We also honor our teachers and we honor our friends.

We don't think it is strange for a mother to keep a child from playing with matches. We know, that matches can be dangerous. But the child does not yet know this, and has to be watched and taught. So the child must learn to honor his mother's wishes when she says, "No!" At each stage of our growing up, there are dangers of this kind that we don't see until we grow older. That is why we must respect and honor the advice of those who are watching us, whether parents, teachers, or even friends.

Man is small

And just as there is much that the child does not understand, so there is an infinity of things that man does not understand.

We have learned how wondrous man is. Now we must think about how small man is. Each of us has felt this when looking upward at the vastness of the sky, especially at night, seeing the moon and the stars. Today, man is beginning to probe the sky and to reach into space, but even as he does so, it becomes ever-larger and deeper beyond him.

In a poem in the Bible, our forefathers expressed this feeling.

"When I behold Thy heavens, the work of Thy fingers, the moon and the stars, which Thou hast established, what is man that Thou art mindful of him?"

For isn't it strange that this speck of dust, this man, is in the mind of God?

Adam was made of the dust of the earth. Even his name tells us so, for "adamah" is the Hebrew word for earth. And to remind us how small is man, the Rabbis asked a question about creation: "Why was man created last?" Some said, to show that man was most important. But others gave the opposite answer. If man becomes haughty, he should remember that even the tiniest fly was created ahead of him!

We have reminded ourselves of all the wonders man has learned to do. But far, far greater are the things we cannot do. We cannot put life back into a dead creature. We cannot make time go backward. We cannot make time stand still.

To keep this always in mind is to have humility. We must remember the words of the prophet Micah, which became a creed for each Jew, "to do justly, to love mercy and to walk humbly with thy God."

It is the word "humbly" that tells so much for humanity. We have examples of its meaning from the earliest wisdom of our people. "Why," the Rabbis asked, "did God speak to Moses from a lowly bush, instead of from a tall tree, or even from the clouds?" God chose the bush so as to show that the lowliest of plants was worthy of the greatest honor.

King Solomon and the ant

In the stories of King Solomon we are shown how even this wisest of kings had to learn not to be too proud. King Solomon learned this lesson from the lowly ants.

One day he was marching with his army through the valley of the ants, when he heard one ant order all the others to move out of the way so as not to be crushed. Solomon halted, and summoned the ant who had spoken. "Who are you?" he asked. She replied "I am the queen of the ants."

"Ah," said King Solomon. "Now, I want to ask you a question."

She refused to answer, unless he took her up on the palm of his hand. He did this, and then he asked, "Is there anyone greater than I am in all the world?"

"Yes," said the ant.

"Who?" demanded Solomon.

"I am!" said the ant.

"What!" cried Solomon. "How is that possible?"

"Were I not greater than you," said the ant, "then God would not have led you to march all the way here, just to put me on your hand!"

"What!" cried Solomon, throwing the ant to the ground, "Do you know who I am? I am King Solomon, the son of David the king!"

"And kingdoms come and kingdoms have gone," said the ant, "and dust thou art, and to dust thou must return! And better were it that thou didst not boast, but remember that in the face of God's eternity, thy kingdom is no greater than an anthill."

Then Solomon went on his way, a humble man.

What we have learned so far

If we always keep in mind how limited we are, then we will not become too proud. We will not expect ourselves, or anyone else, to be perfect. We will look at all other people, and respect them, because they are just as special as we are, and we have just the same limits as they have.

To keep this balance of wonder and of modesty means to know our true value in the world. Each speck of dust is a marvel of wonders, and yet it is a speck of dust.

QUESTIONS TO THINK ABOUT

1. Man is both a "crown of creation" and a "speck in the universe." Can you give other examples of how important man is at one time and how unimportant at another time?

2. How do we show our respect for God when we keep our bodies clean? What story did Hillel tell to explain this idea?

QUESTIONS TO ASK YOUR PARENTS

1. Sometimes parents treat their children as if they were very important and at other times as if they were very unimportant. Can your parents explain to you why they act this way? Can you decide when there is a "healthy balance" between the two in your family?

2. Can you tell your parents how a lowly bush taught Moses and a tiny ant taught Solomon that small things can also be very important? Can you or your parents think of any other lowly or tiny things that show us the wonder of God's world?

CHAPTER XVII

Honesty Is the Right Way

When Hitler decided to attack Poland and start the great World War, he ordered about twenty men from his own side to be dressed in Polish uniforms. He had them killed, and left on a field in front of a German radio station near the Polish border. Then he screamed to the whole world that the Poles had attacked a German radio station. And with this excuse, he started the war by ordering his army to march into Poland.

Of course, all this was a lie. It was a lie with fake "evidence"—the bodies of his own men, dressed up in Polish uniforms. And it was unjust; the Poles had done nothing against him. But his armies were standing ready to march into Poland and destroy the Poles.

Lying and injustice go together

Thus, lying and injustice and war all came together.

Our Rabbis long ago saw this. They had a saying that "the world rests on three things: justice, truth, and peace." And they said, "All three are one, because where there is no truth there can be no justice, and where there is no justice there is no peace."

How many times have you seen a fight start because two boys were arguing, maybe about a baseball that one of them found.

"It's mine! I lost it right near there!"

"You're a liar!"

"You are! You stole it!"

And soon they are fighting. That won't prove who was lying. It will only prove who is stronger.

Often it is very hard, almost impossible, to prove the truth. And yet, how can there be justice, if someone is lying? And we already know that without justice people cannot live together in a group. Everyone has the same right to life, and this means every person has the right to the truth from other people.

If people lie, it is impossible to have

109

justice. We know the story about the coins in the hollow cane, meaning "the truth will always come out." But often there is much suffering before the truth comes out. Sometimes an innocent man goes to prison for years, because someone has lied.

People lie because it often seems an easy way to get what they want. The lie is the favorite whisper of the *yetzer ha-ra*. And the hardest work of justice is to struggle against lies. Everyone has heard the famous story about King Solomon, how he found which of two women was telling the truth. It is the story of the two women who came to him with one baby, each saying the baby was hers. King Solomon said, "Let a sword be brought." And then he said, "I will divide the baby in two, and give each an equal share." One woman cried out, "No, no, don't hurt it! Let her have it!" And so Solomon knew she was the true mother, while the other had been lying.

Honesty makes us feel good

Not every judge can have Solomon's genius for finding out who is lying. Today, we even have machines to help us. There is a machine called the lie detector, which registers what happens inside a person while he is answering questions. Sometimes it shows a difference in his heartbeat that tells us that probably the person is lying. One cannot always be sure about this.

But most people feel uneasy when they lie—and even if they can control their expression, and even if they can look you straight in the eye, something inside them is not the same.

But when we tell the truth—even where a lie would be easy—we have a peaceful feeling inside, and we are proud of ourselves. Peace with ourselves, as well as peace in the world, depends on truthfulness and honesty.

There is one word we use both for liars and for thieves. We say someone is dishonest, because these things usually go together. If a thief is caught, he tries to lie his way out of it. He tries to prove he was somewhere else when the theft happened. To lie is

Solomon said, "Let a sword be brought."

to steal; for, when you lie, you are stealing someone's trust in you.

The eighth Commandment tells us, "Thou shalt not steal." And of course, just as the liar is uneasy, the thief is uneasy. There is a Jewish saying about a stolen cap: "The stolen cap burns on the thief's head." This means that every time someone looks at him, the thief imagines the person is looking at his hat. He begins to feel as if his head is on fire.

But a real thief is not likely to go around wearing the cap he has stolen. He sells what he steals. What happens, then, if the owner of the cap sees it being worn by someone who bought it without knowing it was stolen?

Our laws, which go back to the ancient Jewish laws, say that the person who bought stolen goods, even if he did not know they were stolen, must give them back to the first owner.

Indeed, not only what is stolen, but what is lost, should be given back to the owner, if we know to whom it belongs. "Finders keepers" is true only if we cannot find out who is the real owner.

One of the favorite stories about finders, is about a rabbi named Simon ben Shetah, who earned his living by combing out flax. The rabbi's friends wanted to help him, so they bought him a donkey to carry things. And on the saddle of the donkey, the rabbi found a pearl. "From now on you don't have to work so hard," his friends said. "See, we bought you a donkey, and you found a precious pearl on it!" He said to them, "Does the owner know of this?" "No," they said. "Go, and give the pearl to him!" the rabbi cried.

Holding back truth is like telling a lie

To know something that another person should know and not to tell it, is as bad as telling a lie. The Bible tells us many times, how wrong such things are. "Ye shall not steal, neither deal falsely, nor lie to one another," is in the laws of Moses. "Keep thee far from lying," we are told, and "Speak ye every man the truth with his neighbor."

The ninth Commandment tells us, "Thou shalt not bear false witness against thy neighbor." This means not to lie about other people in court or at a trial, for then we are not only telling a lie, but telling a lie to prevent justice!

One lie leads to another

The person who lies usually has to tell other lies to cover up the first one, and soon he is caught up in a web of lies. Sometimes the first lie is almost innocent. Suppose David comes home with his jacket torn and soiled. Mother asks what happened. He doesn't want to admit he has been fighting again, so he lies. "I fell," he says. Mother asks whether he got hurt, and he says no. But she is worried, and she examines his jacket and sees some spots. "Are those blood stains?" she asks. David doesn't want to admit he got a bloody nose, and he can't admit it now anyway, so he lies some more. "It's red paint," he says. And Mother asks, "What were you doing with red paint?" So he makes up another one, "We were painting in school." "What did you paint?" And so he must tell more lies. He doesn't like himself for telling lies, and he gets angry and shouts at his mother, "Don't ask so many questions!" And so the trouble begins.

And when everybody finds out a person is in the habit of lying, nobody believes him even when he tells the truth. We see this in the story of the shepherd who cried "Wolf, wolf," all the time, even when there was no wolf. Then when a wolf really came, nobody paid any attention to his shouting.

Cheating, slander and gossip are like lies

As we know, there are ways of lying without lying out loud. Cheating is a

One lie must be piled on another

Passing on tales about another is gossip

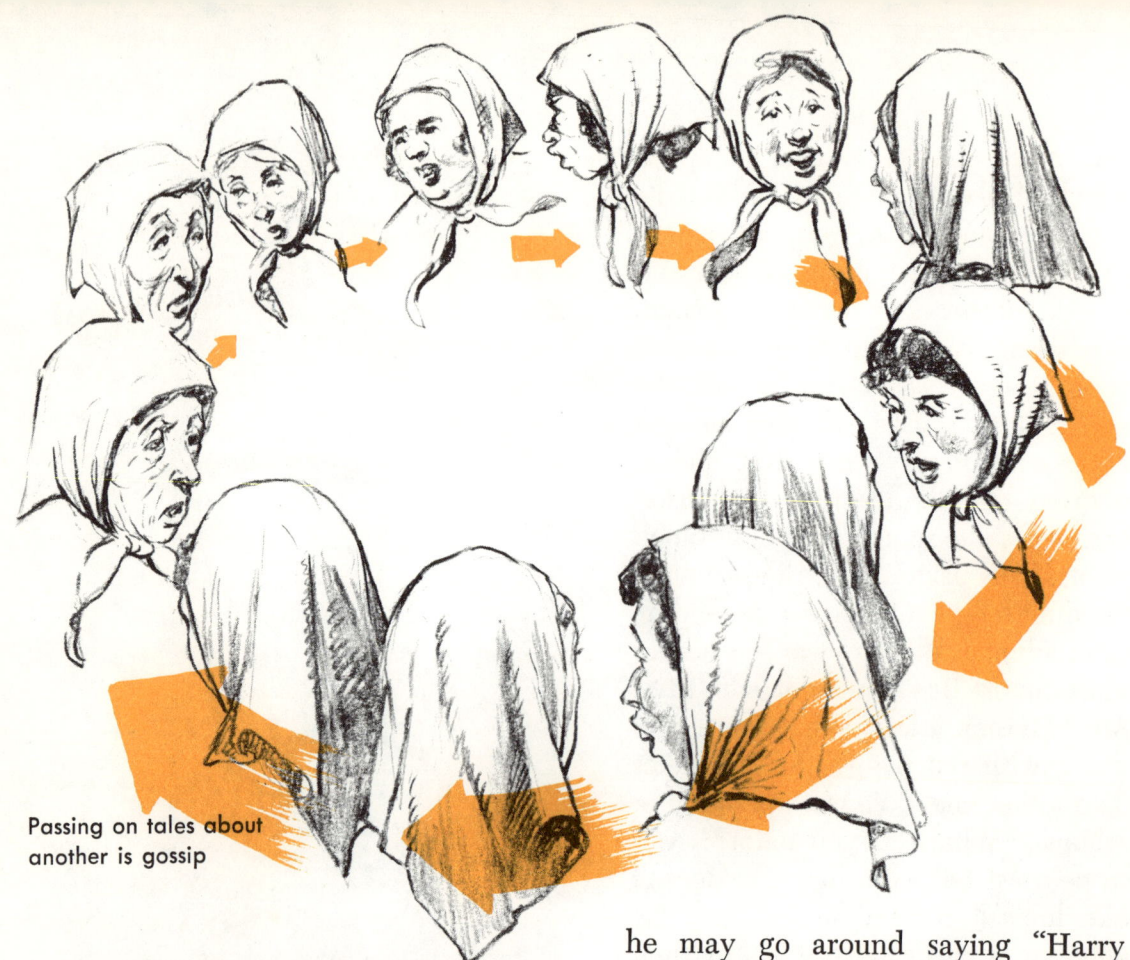

combination of lying and stealing. If you cheat in a test at school and get a good mark, you don't gain anything, because later on you will miss what you were supposed to have learned. If someone cheats in a game and wins, he knows he has not really won, and the fun is gone. If he got a prize for being the winner, then he has really become a thief by stealing the prize.

The *yetzer ha-ra* has many other ways of suggesting dishonesty to us. Slander is one of them. Telling a mean lie about a person, in order to hurt him, is slander. For instance, if John is jealous of Harry's good marks, he may go around saying "Harry cheats. I saw him." That is slander.

Next to slander comes gossip. David may hear John's remark about Harry's cheating, and even if he hardly knows Harry, David may pass the same story on to others. This is gossip.

Flattery and bribery are like lies

Another form of lying is to pretend to be something one is not. We often see this in school. A boy may pretend to be a little angel when the teacher's eyes are on him, but as soon as her back is turned, he talks and fights and causes trouble. Pretending to be what you are not is called hypocrisy. The exception to this is when you pretend in a play or in a game. Then, of course, it is fun. But pretending in order to deceive people is dishonest.

Another way of being dishonest with people is by flattery. Suppose Mary doesn't like Jane. But she wants to be invited to Jane's party, so she starts telling Jane her clothes are lovely, and says, "I like you better than any girl in the class." That is flattery.

Flattery is really a kind of bribery. But bribery goes further. It means offering a person something he wants, to make him do something he might not choose to do. Suppose John wants to be class president. He may tell one of his classmates, "If you vote for me, I'll make you a monitor." He may tell another, "Vote for me and I'll help you in the examinations." This is bribery.

Bribery is one of the worst things. If a thief is caught, he will sometimes offer money to the policeman to let him go. Sometimes even a respectable citizen who gets a speeding ticket will offer money to a policeman to tear up the ticket. That, too, is bribery. And it is just as wrong to offer a bribe as to take one, because both are ways of cheating justice.

What we have learned so far

When people get used to injustice and lying, they may very well end up in fighting and in war. Stealing and lying and cheating, and all forms of dishonesty are wrong. We know this in our hearts. All these things are unfair to other people, and they make us unhappy and uncomfortable with ourselves. When we are honest, we feel good. We feel that we can face everyone eye to eye, and we can face God.

QUESTIONS TO THINK ABOUT

1. Sometimes a small lie leads a person to tell a bigger lie so he won't have to admit that he told a lie in the first place. Do you remember when this ever happened to you or to someone you know?

2. Cheating is described in this chapter as a form of lying and stealing. Did you ever hear anyone defend himself when he admitted that he cheated? What did you think of his excuse?

QUESTIONS TO ASK YOUR PARENTS

1. Police sometimes use a machine called a "lie detector" when they want to find out if someone is telling the truth. Ask your parents if they know when you are telling the truth if they ask you a question about some wrong thing they think you may have done.

2. Ask your parents to give you examples of why flattery, slander and bribery are as dishonest as stealing. Use the examples given in this chapter to explain this idea.

CHAPTER XVIII

Repentance and Forgiveness Are the Right Ways

There is a story of modern times, called "The Assistant." It is about a young man in Brooklyn, who was hanging around with a tough fellow and went with him to rob a grocery store. It was only a little store in a poor neighborhood, and the storekeeper was an old Jew who scarcely made a living.

The grocer was putting away the few dollars he had taken in that day when the two boys came to the back of the store to rob him. The Jew was so surprised that he began to yell, and then the tough boy hit him on the head with a club. The storekeeper fell down, bleeding. The boys took his cash and ran away.

The tough fellow didn't care what he had done. But the other boy got very upset when he heard the storekeeper was very sick from the blows on his head. The boy stayed around that little street in Brooklyn, and when the grocer was able to open his store again, he asked if he needed an assistant. The storekeeper couldn't afford to pay a helper, so the boy said he was willing to work for just his food and a place to sleep in back of the shop. He kept coming every day, and helping a little, till the grocer said, "All right."

The young man proved such a good helper, so friendly and smiling to the customers, that soon business began to get better, and the storekeeper was able to pay him.

But even when things were going well, the young man didn't feel quite right. He didn't feel right until one day he told the storekeeper, "You know that time you were held up? I was one of the boys who robbed you."

This story has a happy ending. The "assistant" married the storekeeper's daughter.

It is a story of repentance. The hold-up man more than gave back the money he had taken, when he worked for the storekeeper. He could not take away the days and nights of pain of that broken head. However, he could make things a little more right by admitting what he did to the man he had hurt, so the man could see he was truly sorry and would never rob anyone again.

We can repent for the bad things we do

Often we do things or say things we are sorry for. We say something we wish we could take right back. Or we do something we wish we could undo.

It isn't always enough simply to say, "I take it back," or simply to say, "I'm sorry." Suppose you are just playing, and by accident, as you get a little too rough, one of your playmates falls in the mud. You will try to clean him off, and say, "I'm sorry, I really didn't mean it," and you'll tell yourself you'll be more careful the next time. Maybe he will try to push you into the mud and say, "See how you like it!" or maybe everything will pass off without trouble. People are not angels. When we do something wrong without meaning to, we can apologize. A sincere apology is the main part of setting things right. The second part is to mend what is damaged or replace it, and to try not to be so careless again. You could offer to have the boy's muddy clothes cleaned.

Judaism teaches us that God will forgive us if we truly repent for the wrongs we have done.

As the Rabbis say, "Better is one hour of repentance and good deeds in

We can apologize and help set things right

117

this world, than the whole life in the world to come."

There are four steps in repentance

This saying tells us that repentance must be joined by "good deeds." There are really four steps in righting a wrong. The first is to admit to ourselves that we have done something wrong. We must feel truly sorry.

The second step is to admit it to the person who was wronged or hurt.

The third step is to make up for the damage done. This is not always simple. Suppose you gossip about someone and spread bad stories that hurt that person. It is not always easy to "take it all back." Suppose you break someone's keepsake. It is impossible to replace a keepsake with something "just as good." But if you are sincerely sorry and try to make things up in other ways, the person will understand.

The fourth step in righting a wrong is a long one. It means trying never to do the same wrong thing again.

As our Rabbis explained, "A man who sins, repents, and then commits the same sin again is like a person with a muddy snake in his hands who washes himself clean, but then he

1. ADMITTING MISTAKE TO OURSELVES

2. ADMITTING IT TO WRONGED PERSON

The four steps in repentance

picks up the muddy snake again. He is still not clean."

Whenever we can, we must take all four steps to repair a wrong. Suppose a child steals a candy bar in a store. He must understand that he has done something wrong and feel sorry. But this is not enough. Of course he must return the candy bar or pay for it. But he must not pretend that he just "forgot to pay." The hardest part is to tell the storekeeper what he did. Surprisingly, it may turn out afterward to be the part he feels best about, and the storekeeper may be as proud of him as he is of himself. And then he must resolve never to do anything of the sort again. Only then has he fully repented.

It is not always possible to do all four things. For example, suppose a boy lets the air out of a tire on a parked car. Later he is sorry he did this. Indeed, someone may have done the same thing to his father's car, and he may see how much trouble this makes. But he doesn't know who owned the car he picked on, so he can't tell the owner he is sorry. And he can't put air back in that tire. All he can do is decide never to be so mean again. And perhaps it will help

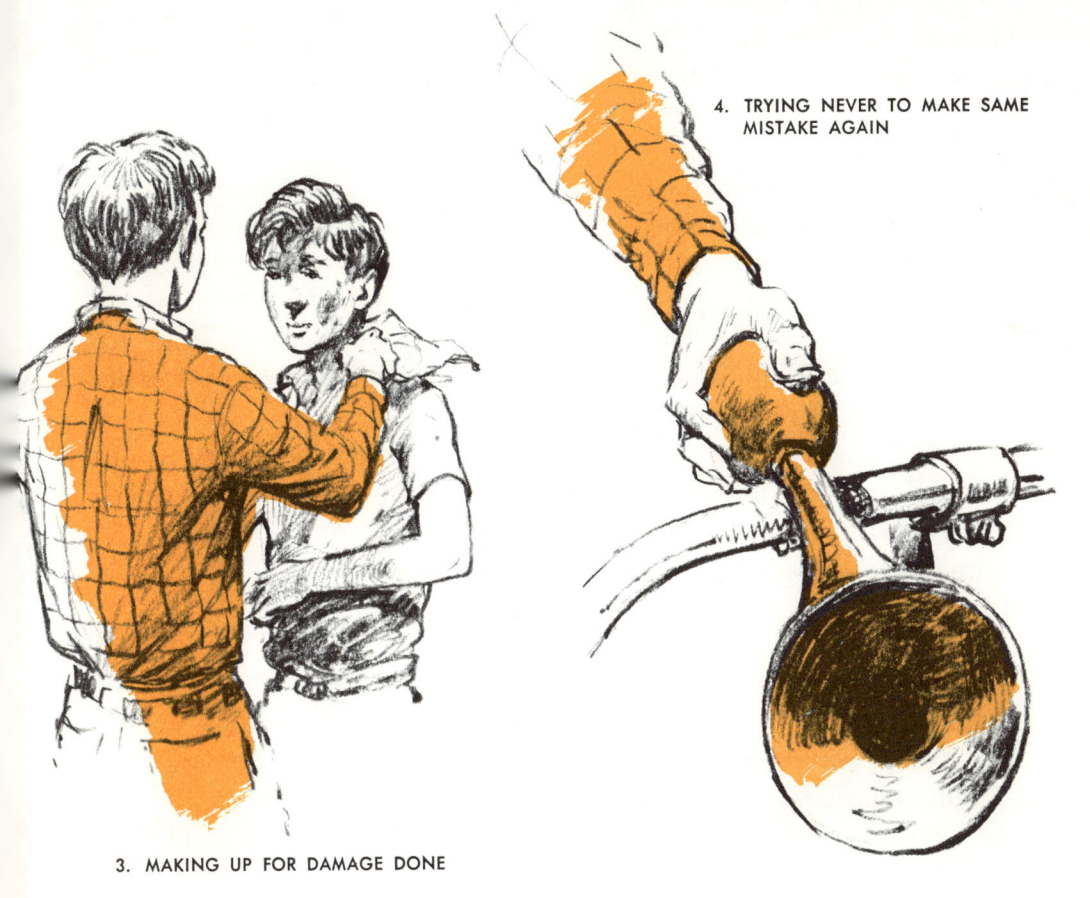

4. TRYING NEVER TO MAKE SAME MISTAKE AGAIN

3. MAKING UP FOR DAMAGE DONE

him if he admits to his parents that he played such a mean nasty trick.

God forgives us if we truly repent

Everybody listens sometimes to his *yetzer ha-ra*. The Bible tells us, "There is not a righteous man upon earth, who doeth good, and sinneth not." In fact, when people are too good, they make us uncomfortable. They don't seem human!

God knows what man is like and does not expect man to be perfect. He only expects us to do as little wrong as possible, and to be sincerely sorry when we have done something wrong. He wants us to repent, and to make amends.

In Hebrew, the word for repentance is *teshuvah*. It means "return." It means to come back to God. In Judaism, we have one day of the year when we think of all the wrong things we have done, and pray for forgiveness, and repent. This is Yom Kippur, the Day of Atonement.

God forgives us if we truly repent. The Rabbis show us God's forgiveness in this story of a king and his son: A king had a son who had gone astray. The boy had gone to a wicked city, a hundred days' journey from his home. And when friends found him and said, "Return home to your father, he will forgive you," he said, "I cannot." Then the father sent word to his son, saying, "Return only as far as you can, and I will come to you the rest of the way."

The Rabbis pointed out the moral. If you repent and return to God, He will return to you.

When we are truly sorry, and have done our best to make amends, then we know that God forgives us, and also people forgive us. Then we are able to forgive ourselves, and feel fresh, and new, and better. We understand that other people are as good as we are. So if they are sorry when they do wrong, and if they try to make up for it, we forgive them, just as we want to be forgiven when we repent.

What we have learned so far

We know that even the most horrible crimes can be forgiven, if repentance is true. Cain was guilty of the most horrible crime. He killed his own

Yom Kippur, the Day of Atonement

brother. He could not bring Abel to life again. But even Cain was forgiven, because he repented.

We have learned the steps we must take in order to repent. We understand that if we are truly sorry, God is always ready to forgive us. And man, who is made in the image of God, must follow in His way, and forgive other people too when they sincerely regret their wrongs.

QUESTIONS TO THINK ABOUT

1. Do you remember when you did something wrong and when you were forgiven because you apologized? Did you ever forgive someone who apologized to you for doing a wrong thing to you? Give examples of both.

2. We are told in this chapter that everyone sins at some time. On which Jewish holiday do we ask forgiveness for the sins we all commit? Why do we expect to be forgiven for these sins?

QUESTIONS TO ASK YOUR PARENTS

1. Explain to your parents the four steps necessary to right a wrong as described in this chapter. Discuss with your parents how you could follow these four steps in asking forgiveness for something you did recently.

2. The Bible tells us that God forgave Cain even though Cain killed his brother Abel. Ask your parents if this story can be used to prove that no murderer should ever be killed as a punishment.

CHAPTER XIX

Hillel's Rule Is the Right Way

It seems awfully complicated at times to know what is the right thing to do. Sometimes it sounds as though we should follow opposite pieces of advice at the same time. We should believe in ourselves, and yet we should be humble. We should always tell the truth, but we should never hurt people's feelings. We should be peaceful, but we shouldn't let somebody hit us without defending ourselves.

So what is right and what is wrong?

This seems to be a very complicated question. People have been writing laws about it for thousands of years. How can anyone ever know all those rules?

Isn't there a simple way to know what is right and what is wrong?

Yes, there is, and every child knows the simple test. Indeed, every child is likely to discover this test for himself. When somebody runs up from behind you and pushes you into a snowbank, what do you say? You most likely would say, "How would you like it if I did it to you?" When somebody tries to get in ahead of the line at the movies, everybody yells, "There's a line here! How would you like it if someone pushed in ahead of you?"

This is the test that was taught by our great sages.

They taught us that everyone *does know* what is right and what is wrong. That the spark of God in us tells us what is right. But we don't always let ourselves believe what we know, and our Rabbis and our sages and our parents have to teach us, to guide us, and show us the right way to follow.

The Bible's simple rule

The Bible put this rule into three Hebrew words, which we translate into five English words, "Love thy neighbor as thyself." By "neighbor," the Bible means any other person, whether we know him or not.

See how simple this is, and yet how nothing is left out! If the Bible only said, "Love thy neighbor," without saying "as thyself," then we might not understand the important lesson of equality, and also miss the reminder of self-respect that is in those few words.

Hillel's rule

Now, there is another way of saying the same thing, that makes it easy to test almost every urge that we have, so as to know whether it is an urge from the *yetzer ha-ra* or the *yetzer ha-tov*.

This test comes from the words of the beloved rabbi and teacher, Hillel. In Jerusalem, there were two great colleges of Judaism. One was the school of Hillel, and the other was the school of Shammai. And they were rivals, perhaps like Yale and Harvard.

The story is told of a heathen, a simple man who couldn't read or write and didn't have a head for learning and was a bit impatient, too. He came to Shammai and said, "I will believe in your God if you can teach me the whole Torah while I stand on one foot."

Shammai thought this man was making fun of the Torah. He drove him away with a rod that he had in his hand. Then the man went to Hillel and asked the same question. And he lifted up one foot.

Hillel answered, "Do not do to your fellow man what you hate to have done unto you."

When the surprised heathen put his foot down, Hillel said, "That is the whole Torah, the rest is commentary. Now go and study."

This is the test that we give, when

we say, "How would you like it if I did it to you?"

And if we have an urge to lie to someone, or to take his pen without asking, or to get ahead of him in line, we can simply ask ourselves, "How would I like it if he did it to me?"

"The great rule of the Torah"

Our great teachers and rabbis had many times reminded people of this test. Rabbi Akiba, who became a martyr when the Romans ruled Judea, always pointed out to people the line in the Bible that says, "Love thy neighbor as thyself," and told them this was the "great rule of the Torah." Many religions have the same rule, in different words. The Christians have the Golden Rule, which says, "Do unto others as you would have others do unto you."

If we use this simple test, everything we have learned really explains itself.

Since we don't want others to be unfair to us, we ought not to be unfair to them. For we all want justice.

Since we want others to be loving and kind and helpful to us, we ought to be helpful to them, and treat them with love and kindness.

Since we want others to share with us, we ought to share with them.

Since we don't want others to lie and steal from us, we begin by being truthful and honest.

Do we want others to respect us? Then we ought to respect them.

Since we want others to be sorry when they hurt us, and not to repeat the hurt, then we must be sorry when we hurt them and we must not repeat our wrong.

Do we want others to forgive us? Then we must forgive them.

Each of us may feel at times that what he does or does not do is strictly his own affair. Yet we have a saying, "We are all in the same boat." This saying goes back to a story told in Jerusalem by Rabbi Simon ben Yochai. "Suppose there are a number of men in a boat," he said, "and one man takes a drill and begins to bore a hole beneath him. His companions say, 'What are you doing?' He answers, 'What affair is it of yours? I am not boring the hole under your seat, I am boring it only under my seat.' They answer, 'It is our affair, because the water will come in and swamp the whole boat, with us in it.'"

If each person lived by Hillel's Rule, then all persons and nations would live by it, and we would have a perfect world. But we know that not even one person can be perfect, much less a whole nation of people.

If people and nations lived by Hillel's Rule, then there would be no hatred between people of different religions, since they all have a version of the same rule. There would be no hatred between people of different colors or different countries. People would respect and trust each other. Nations would trust each other instead of being afraid of each other. There would be no wars. There would be no starving people because those who had too much would share with those who had too little.

Israel is a tiny country without enough food, but it is learning how to raise crops, even under bad conditions. And, since it has no extra food to give away, Israel is sending out experts to teach what they have learned to people in Africa and Asia, where the soil is also poor.

There would be peace in the world

We pray for peace with every prayer, for peace is the great ideal of Judaism. Even when we only say "Hello" in Hebrew, we say "Shalom," which means peace. And when we say "Goodbye," we say the same word, "Shalom." The name of the holy city Jerusalem, means "City of Peace."

The prophet Isaiah also saw the importance of peace. He spoke of the time when "nation will not lift up sword against nation," and even "the wolf and the lamb will live together and the leopard will lie down with the kid." No one of us alone can bring the great time of peace, but we believe that this is the great design of God, and that mankind is slowly helping in this design, as people try to become better.

Our actions make a difference

Each wrong thing we do holds back the perfection of the design.

Suppose it is only a little thing, such as we see any day in class. The class has been very noisy. The teacher asks everyone to be quiet while she writes on the blackboard. As soon as her back is turned, David whispers to his neighbor. The teacher turns and asks, "Who spoke?" No one answers. She says, "Unless the child who spoke will raise his hand, the whole class will be kept after school."

No one will tattle on David. And he can be silent and let the whole class be punished for what he did. Or he can do the right thing and raise his hand. In that case he may be kept after school, but the rest of the class will not suffer. Some mothers who are waiting outside will not be kept

What we do is not always only our affair

longer. Children who have other things to do, like going to the dentist, or taking music lessons, or playing baseball, will do them. And David will feel better inside himself.

He will not have listened to his *yetzer ha-ra*. But to do right, does not mean only to stay away from doing wrong. Our *yetzer ha-tov* tells us helpful things to do all the time. Suppose it has snowed and the sidewalks are covered. David is shoveling the snow in front of his own house. He knows that the woman next door, who lives alone, is too old to shovel the snow. So he cleans off her walk for her.

His thoughtfulness has made David a better person. He feels good, and he will want to do other things that make him feel good in this same way. Just as we learned that one lie leads to another, so the *Ethics of the Fathers* teaches us that "one good deed leads to another."

What we have learned so far

The more we follow Hillel's great rule, "Do not do to your fellow man what you hate to have done unto you," the closer we bring the world toward peace.

We know that we are not perfect and the world will not be perfect in our days. But the *Ethics of the Fathers* tells us of a saying of Rabbi Tarfon. "Even though it is not in our power to finish the work, we are not free to give it up altogether."

We are not free to give up the work. Each of us is part of God's plan. And each of us wants to do the most he can to help make a beautiful and peaceful world.

QUESTIONS TO THINK ABOUT

1. Sometimes it is hard to tell when something is right and when it is wrong. Suppose you were in the class which had to be kept after school because David would not admit to the teacher that he was the one who was talking. Would it be right for you to tell the teacher? Is it right for David not to admit it and to allow the whole class to be punished? How would you explain Hillel's rule to David?

2. The story of a man drilling a hole in a boat is a good example of how we are "all in the same boat." Can you think of another example?

QUESTIONS TO ASK YOUR PARENTS

1. Ask your parents if they ever felt sad because things did not get better no matter how hard they tried. Explain to them the saying of Rabbi Tarfon: "Even though it is not in our power to finish the work, we are not free to give it up altogether."

2. A Jewish writer once wrote that Hillel's saying "Do *not* do to your fellow man what you hate to have done unto you" is a better guide than the Golden Rule which says "*Do* unto others as you would have others *do* unto you." Ask your parents to help explain what the writer may have had in mind.

UNIT FIVE

What Judaism Teaches Us About Life

CHAPTER XX

The World We Live in Is Good

What do we mean when we say we have faith in someone? We mean we know that person is good and we trust him no matter what he does. Even if we don't understand exactly what he is doing, we know he would not do it unless it were right and good.

This is what some religions mean by faith in God. They mean that we must believe in God and trust him, knowing that He is good and that everything will be right in the end.

Life is good

In Judaism, this is our faith too. But we believe even more. We not only believe that goodness will come in the end. We believe that the world is good all the time and that the life of man on earth is good.

We see that there is suffering and injustice on earth, and our Rabbis spoke a great deal about the reward "in the world to come." Yet, before everything else, Judaism tells us that God wants us to enjoy all that is good in this life on earth.

Each of us knows this in the feeling that comes on a beautiful morning when we wake up after a good sleep and see the sun coming in through the windows. We take a deep breath; the air is sweet; we stretch; and we feel like singing out in joy, "How *good* the world is! How good it is to be alive!"

The world God made is good

That is when we feel in our own hearts the great truth that is written among the very first lines in the Bible. The Bible tells us that the world God made is good. Again and again, these words come to us in the first chapter of the story of creation. The very first thing that God made was light.

"And God saw the light, that it was good . . ."

God made the earth, and gathered the water into the seas. "And God saw that it was good."

The earth brought forth grass, and the trees bore fruit, and their seed was in the fruit, each of its own kind.

... "And God saw that it was good."

God made the two great lights, the sun and moon in the sky, to rule over day and night, "And God saw that it was good." God created the whales and all the creatures of the waters and the winged creatures of the air, "And God saw that it was good." God made the creatures of the earth, cattle, and all the other animals that move on the earth, "And God saw that it was good."

And finally, "God saw everything that He had made, and behold, it was very good."

Our teachers and Rabbis studied the meaning of every single word in the Bible. Why was this word used and not another? Why was a certain word used again and again?

Why was the word "good" used so many times in creation? And why was the third day of creation considered to be the luckiest? Because, for the third day, "good" was used twice! On that day, God called the dry land "earth," and gathered the water into the seas, "And God saw that it was good." The earth brought forth grass, and the trees bore fruit, "And God saw that it was good."

And so the third day of the week is considered a day of double-goodness, a lucky day to start a journey, or move into a new house, or start new work.

And then, as they studied each word, our Rabbis saw that at the end of the sixth day of creation, when God saw everything He had made, He saw that it was very good. For now He saw all creation together, the stars in their firmament, and the earth and the seas, and all the creatures in the water and on the earth and in the skies. And He saw that their harmony and unity were more than the goodness of each thing in itself. Now it was *very good!*

We can see for ourselves how very good it is. We see the harmonious

Life is good

We can see the harmonious beauty of the world

beauty of the world each time we lift our eyes to it.

We feel the sun reaching down to our earth and to our bodies, reaching to warm us and to warm the earth and to stir the seeds in the earth that provide us with our food. How amazing it is! Through all that distance, the sun's warmth comes at just the right temperature to melt the winter snows and send fresh water down through a million streams to wet the seeds in the earth.

And in the heat of day, the same water freshens us and quenches our thirst, too, and moves into all the cells of our bodies to make us live.

Life is holy

Life comes directly from God. Life is holy. Therefore we may not destroy life.

Judaism teaches us that murder is a crime against God and suicide, too, is a crime against God, because for man to kill another man is to destroy the highest of God's creations.

It is as though man were setting himself above God!

God is the source of life, and although man has learned a great deal about how our body works, and how chemistry works, still man cannot know the making of life itself.

In ancient times, people believed the source of life was in our blood, for they could see the body die when its blood flowed out. Therefore Jews, who knew that life itself is holy, were not allowed to eat or drink blood. Not even the blood of an animal, not even a blood-specked egg. For blood meant life, and life is holy.

In Judaism, almost every rule may be broken in order to save life, which is holy. The strict rules of the Sabbath and even of Yom Kippur are set aside if a life is in danger. Sabbath is our holy day of rest, but even among the Jews who most strictly keep to this rule, a doctor may go to a stricken person on Sabbath.

On Yom Kippur, we fast. But if a person is weak, or sick, and a doctor tells him he must eat or drink, he not only *may* take this nourishment on the day of the fast, but he *must* do it, in order to preserve his life.

We know how good the world is through the wondrous ability of our bodies. God created man with a million complicated wonders, so that man can enjoy all the goodness of creation. We stand and walk upright, our Rabbis told us, so that our feet are on the earth, and our heads are toward heaven.

We have five senses—to touch, smell, see, hear, taste the wonders of the world. We have a way to mingle all that these senses tell us, to put all this together into feelings of joy and love.

We have the gift of imagination to use our wonderful bodies, so that they can do so much more than is needed only to exist. With our limbs, we not only move about and make things, but we dance, we leap, we dive. We not only speak, but we sing and whistle and laugh. We use our bodies joyously, and to use our bodies well gives us joy.

God is always near

Sometimes this comes to us so strongly that we feel we will burst with happiness in God's beautiful, wonderful world. Those are moments when we feel that without any explanation we understand it all. Those are moments of ecstasy. And there was a time not long ago—only a few hundred years—when this feeling of joy and ecstasy swept through a large part of the Jewish world.

Most Jews were then living in Europe—in Poland and Russia. And a holy man in a small town, a rabbi called the Baal Shem Tov, began to teach Jews to pray with joy. His followers were called *Hassidim*. Many people had thought of the Jewish religion as a religion of rules and study. But now, as if a door had been opened, the feeling of joy was released. "God's goodness is everywhere!" the Hassidim cried. They felt so close to God, that sometimes instead of speaking to God as "Thee" or "Thou" they spoke to Him very familiarly, as "Du," or "You." A favorite Hassidic song went, "Du, Du, Du," and was called a "Dudaleh!"

Wherever I go—it's You!
Wherever I stand—it's You!
And only You, and You again, and
   always You,
   Du-Du-Du-Du-Du!

If all is well—it's You!
If trouble comes—we turn to You!
I look there—it's You!
I look here—it's You!
And only You, and You again, and
   always You,
   Du-Du-Du-Du-Du!

Like the Hassidim, we often have this feeling that God is very, very close and that we can trust Him. We feel that God can be reached by everyone and that He listens to the smallest child and even to the worst sinner.

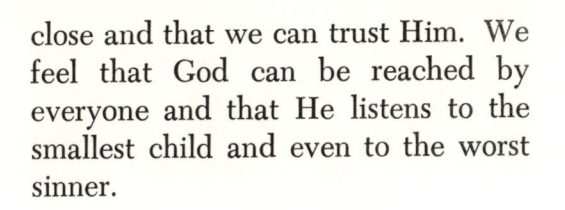

God is fair

Judaism teaches us that God is fair. Our Bible tells us the story of the wicked city of Sodom, so wicked that it had to be destroyed. When Abraham was told about this, he argued with God that it was not fair to destroy the good with the bad. "Shall not the Judge of all the earth do justly?" Abraham said. Suppose there were as many as ten good people in the city, would God not spare it? God agreed that even if there were ten good people, He would spare

Hassidim prayed with joy

Sodom. Since there were not, He destroyed the city. But He spared the only good people—the family of Lot, Abraham's nephew.

God is found within ourselves

Judaism teaches that God loves us and is close to us everywhere. And the Hassidim tell a story to show that this greatest treasure is within ourselves if we will but look for it. The story is about Rabbi Eisek ben Yekel, of the city of Cracow.

One day he dreamed a dream. In it he saw the bridge that stands in the city of Prague and leads to the king's palace. Beneath this bridge, he was told in his dream, he would find a treasure.

After the same dream came a second and a third time, Rabbi Eisek started off on the long way to Prague. He came at last to the palace bridge and saw that soldiers guarded it day and night. So he couldn't dig under the bridge for the treasure. Every morning he came and hung around until night, so that at last the captain of the guard asked him if he were looking for someone or waiting for someone. Rabbi Eisek told him the dream that had brought him from such a great distance. The captain laughed and said, "Imagine walking so far, only because of a dream! If I believed in dreams, I too would have to take a long journey. I once dreamed that I should go to the city of Cracow and find a Jew named Eisek ben Yekel and look for a treasure under his stove! Eisek ben Yekel! Half the Jews in Cracow must be named Eisek, and half of their fathers are named Yekel, so I would have to dig up the whole city!" And he laughed again.

Rabbi Eisek hurried home and dug under his stove—and found a treasure! He built a synagogue and gave it his name, so that Jews shall always remember that even though what they seek seems impossible to find—if they have faith, they will find it closest to home. For the true treasure is always there—the knowledge of God right within ourselves.

What we have learned so far

In the summer air, the birds sing, each with its own song, to glorify the goodness of the world. Our religious poets sang the same melody of joy, in words, "The heavens declare the glory of God," they sang in an ancient psalm, "and the firmament showeth His handiwork!"

The world itself is filled with goodness, with cool waters and delicious fruits, and it is all there to feed the goodness of life. Our life is God's gift of feeling and of knowing, of tasting and of remembering all that is good in the world. And all this treasure is right within ourselves.

QUESTIONS TO THINK ABOUT

1. How does the Bible story of creation tell us that we live in a good world?

2. Because Jews feel that life is good, they taught that any observance of a feast or a fast day may be broken if it is necessary to save a life. Can you tell a story you have read or make up a story to explain this idea?

QUESTIONS TO ASK YOUR PARENTS

1. Tell your parents how the Hassidim taught that God is always very close and that He listens to anyone who calls on Him. Do we ever act as if we believed this? How do we show it?

2. Sometimes people travel very far to seek their fortune when it is right in their own backyard or in their own hearts. Tell the story of Rabbi Eisek ben Yekel and ask your parents to give you an example to show this idea.

CHAPTER XXI

Life Is to Be Enjoyed

When we say we should enjoy life, does it mean we should just have fun? Does it mean just eating ice cream and cake and candy, and playing games, and going to the movies, and having picnics? All this is pleasure. But is it joy?

Suppose you wanted a guitar. You noticed that a person who plays a guitar and sings at a party is usually very popular. So you asked your parents to buy you a guitar. But a good one! The best! Even if it cost a hundred dollars!

Maybe you nagged a bit until they bought you a guitar. Then you took a lesson or two and then stopped because you found that you had to practice a good deal before you could play the guitar.

Now, you had a cousin who borrowed a cheap guitar and practiced until he learned to play. And one day your mother came and said, "If you're not going to use your guitar, I'm just going to give it to your cousin, because your cousin *plays* on it!"

You might wail and moan, but you would also feel that it was right. Because to get joy out of life, we must use life. We must use ourselves, too, for the best that is in us.

Suppose your cousin really has a talent for music. You will see that he is never so happy as when he is playing a song. The more complicated the music, and the better he learns to play it, the happier he feels.

Be yourself!

But this does not mean that you, too, must be a guitar-player in order to find joy. You must find the use for yourself that belongs especially to you. One of the great Hassidic rabbis said this as he was coming to the end of his life. Rabbi Zusya wondered how it would be when he was asked in heaven, what he had done with his life. "I'm not worried about being asked why I was not a Moses," said Rabbi Zusya. "I am only worried that they might ask me why I was not Zusya!"

For he was wondering whether he had really "found himself," whether he had really done all that he could with what was given him in life.

God gives us life, and we should use it and respect it and enjoy it, just as we expect the gifts that we give people to be used and enjoyed. When your parents give you a bicycle, they enjoy seeing you ride it. But also, they expect you to take care of this gift. If you leave it in the rain, they feel you really don't care for the gift. But if they see you polishing your bicycle and decorating it, then they are happy they gave it to you.

Our bodies, our minds, our lives are the gifts of God. We should make the best use of these gifts. We should develop our bodies and our minds. We should try not to spoil our lives or use them in the wrong way; and we should try not to spoil or hurt the lives of other people.

Moderation is a good rule
To get the most joy out of life, we have to learn to use each thing with the greatest skill, but also with moderation. If you learn how to ride a horse, you will notice that the riding master loves his horses and is very careful not to let them be used too much. He keeps track of each one. If you come to the stable and ask for Dandy, the riding master may say, "Dandy has already been out twice this afternoon—that's all for him!" And he will have you choose another horse.

This simple rule is not always easy to follow. We like to eat—yet we know that if we eat too much we get fat, and that this can be very unhealthful. We like to play in the sun. Yet if we overdo it we can get sunburned, and our pleasure can result in pain.

Just as we can have too much of

Moderation is a good rule

a good thing with food or with sunshine, we can care too much about money, even though it can bring us good things. Money can bring us enjoyment; it can bring us fine clothes and cars and homes.

It is perfectly right for us to enjoy all these good things, if we are lucky enough to have them. But we all know that it is wrong to make money our chief aim in life. We are surely not making the most of life if we use it only to get more and more money to buy more and more things only for our pleasure.

Judaism tells us to judge each person by his character, not by his bank account or the kind of car he drives. The girl who has the prettiest clothes is not always the nicest or the best girl in the class. The boy who has the most spending money is not always the worst boy, or the best.

The story of a treasure

There is a story about Elijah, which shows the sensible ideas our Rabbis had about wealth and poverty and about enjoying life. The story is about a rich man who lost all his money and became so poor that he had to work as a farmhand. Once, when he was in the field, Elijah appeared to him, dressed as an Arab. "You are destined to enjoy seven good years," said the Arab. "When do you want them, now, or at the end of your life?"

The good man thought this was a temptation from the devil, so he said, "Go away! You are a wizard!" But three times the Arab came with the same question. And the third time, the man said to himself, "Even though I have lost my fortune, why should I think only bad luck will come to me? If I have good luck, and use it well, there is nothing wrong in it." So like a good man, he told the Arab that he would consult his wife. And when Elijah came again, the man answered, "My wife and I agree that if we are to have good fortune, let it come now." Elijah said, "Go home. Before you cross the threshold, good fortune will have filled your house."

And so it was. The man went home

and discovered that his children had found a treasure in the ground. His wife met him at the door and said, "Now we shall enjoy seven good years. Let us practice as much charity as possible!"

During the seven years they enjoyed life. And they did good all around them. At the end of the seven years, Elijah came and announced to the man that the treasure was now to be taken away. The man said, "Before I accepted the gift, I consulted my wife. Now that it is to be taken away, let me talk to her again and tell her what is happening." Elijah agreed.

The man's wife told him to tell Elijah, "If you can find anyone who will do better with the treasure than we did, we will willingly give it up!" And indeed, God recognized that these people had made the right use of their wealth and told Elijah to grant it to them forever as their property.

We enjoy food and drink

Each of us has a treasure to use and to take proper care of—his own person, his body and soul. We must enjoy the good things of the earth, but sensibly. A nice red apple is good to eat, but if we eat six nice red apples we are going to get sick.

Wine is enjoyable. But the Rabbis had a clever saying about wine. Before drinking it, a man is meek as a lamb. When he drinks wine properly, he is brave as a lion. If he drinks a little too much, he becomes as disgusting as a pig. And if he drinks much too much and gets drunk, he becomes as foolish and ridiculous and dangerous as an ape.

And yet, should we stay away from wine and from apples just because too much is bad? Judaism tells us no. Judaism tells us that avoiding the good things of life is wrong. A famous Rabbi said, "A man will one day have to give an account to God for all the good things which his eyes saw and which he did not taste!"

We enjoy our bodies

God gave us our senses for enjoyment, so long as we do not hurt ourselves, or other people. With our eyes, we see a starry night, a friend's face, snow-covered trees, a circus performance; but we do not use our eyes to peek into someone's window.

With our ears, we hear the music of the flute, the patter of rain, the voice of a friend, the chirping of crickets; but we do not use our ears to listen to conversation that is not meant for us.

With our arms and legs we can dance, hop, skip, run, swim, skate, climb, turn somersaults. Using our bodies to do all these things makes us feel alive and healthy and happy. We can use our limbs to defend ourselves, too, but we do not use them to attack and hurt other people.

We enjoy our minds

It is wrong not to make good use of our minds. The ability to think and learn and remember is a wonderful gift from God to mankind. As we learn more about the world, we enjoy life all the more.

Once a child has learned to read, he can make life easier and safer for himself. He can read a street sign and know where he is. He can find a phone number to call his friends. He can read stories for fun.

He can learn and study about life all around him. He can watch the ants and then read about them to find out how they live and work together in their little community.

By studying and learning, people become scientists and doctors and lawyers and mechanics and inventors. They are able to make life much more enjoyable for themselves and other people, too.

Besides our minds to learn with, we have our hearts to love with. We enjoy the world more when we share our pleasures with those we love—with our brothers and sisters, our friends, our parents. It is not much fun to go on a picnic all alone!

And when sad things happen, we find the sadness lifting if we talk of our trouble with our friends and near ones.

The closest sharing is between husband and wife. When God created Adam, He said, "It is not good that

We enjoy our minds and bodies

141

man should be alone." And so He created Eve. After God had created the first human couple, He blessed them and said, "Be fruitful and multiply." And Judaism constantly reminds us that children are born through the happiness of love between man and woman.

What we have learned so far

God wants us to have joy, through our hearts, our minds, our bodies. When we control ourselves to use God's gifts with care and love, we are showing God, in our way of life itself, how thankful we are, and how truly we appreciate His goodly gift of life.

QUESTIONS TO THINK ABOUT

1. God gave us our senses for enjoyment. Can you tell what you enjoy seeing, hearing, tasting, touching and smelling?

2. We can also enjoy our minds when we learn something we feel is important. What kind of learning do you enjoy most?

QUESTIONS TO ASK YOUR PARENTS

1. Parents like to give gifts which their children will enjoy. Which gifts have been most enjoyed by members of your family?

2. Good things may also cause harm if we have too much of them. In this chapter we learned that too much food will upset our stomach and too much sun will give us a sunburn. Can your parents tell you other good things which can cause us harm if we have too much?

CHAPTER XXII

Trouble Is Part of Life

Many of our Rabbis' stories teach us that our good deeds will be rewarded and that our bad deeds will be punished, either now or sometimes in the future. And we can see in the world around us that, while this is not *always* true, it is most often true. We can see that the decent and good people are the ones who get the most good out of life because their hearts are untroubled.

But even the smallest child knows that some trouble can come to anyone. Just as there is a *yetzer ha-tov* and a *yetzer ha-ra*, the rose has its thorns; the bee, that gives sweet honey, can also sting. We enjoy the rose and try to avoid its thorns. We enjoy honey and try to avoid the bee's sting. We enjoy life, in spite of its troubles.

There are two kinds of troubles. The small troubles of daily life do not deeply touch our hearts. Suppose you want to stay up another hour to watch television, but your mother says "no." You may wail for a while, but you'll soon fall asleep. Or your family plans a picnic and it rains that day. Or your bike gets stolen. These are not tragedies.

But if a person we love dies, we feel the death in our hearts. If there are floods and earthquakes in the world, if there is war and millions of people suffer, we feel the tragedy of such widespread sorrow.

Why we have troubles

From the beginning of time, people have asked, "Why are there troubles and evils in the world?" Judaism gives us some answers. And sometimes there is no answer and the riddle must remain a riddle.

Here are some of the answers:

Some troubles are caused by people who choose to do what is wrong instead of what is right. For instance, a bike gets stolen because someone has chosen to do what was wrong, to steal. There may be some very good excuses. There was a wonderful movie called "The Bicycle Thief" that told the story of a poor man whose bicycle was stolen exactly on the day he got a new job. This job depended on his having a bicycle, since he had to ride around town pasting up posters. He was so desperate, so afraid of losing his job, that he tried to steal another bicycle to replace his own. He got caught, and much trouble followed. We pitied him. And yet, he had done a wrong thing in stealing just because another man stole.

Wars are usually started because of wicked people, like Hitler, who want great power.

Even accidents are often caused by people who choose to do what is wrong—to ignore a rule of driving, to drive too fast, or to be careless in some other way.

Another thing that is sometimes said about the troubles in the world is that they help us appreciate the goodness of life.

After a spoonful of bitter medicine, candy tastes even better. After a dreary rain, the sun seems brighter. After being in bed with the measles, it's wonderful to get up and go outdoors. Even a friendship seems better when we make up after a quarrel.

Troubles sometimes help

Still another answer is that troubles make better people of us. The child who has been left out of a game, understands better the feelings of another child who is left out. He is less likely to leave others out.

Our Bible and our prayers tell us constantly to remember that Jews were once slaves in Egypt, so that we will appreciate freedom and help other people to be free.

Still another answer is that troubles may prove to be blessings in disguise. They can save us from even worse troubles. Polio shots sting for a second. But they keep us from getting polio.

Sometimes we may not even know the great troubles that could have befallen us had we not suffered smaller ones. We are taught this by a tale told by the Rabbis:

Once Rabbi Joseph ben Levi was allowed to go with Elijah on his wanderings, but only on condition that he would not ask for explanations of what he saw happening. They stopped the first night at the cottage of a man and wife whose only possession was a cow. The couple welcomed the wayfarers, gave them the best of their food, and lodged them for the night.

Early in the morning, Rabbi Joseph heard Elijah praying that the cow might die. And indeed, before they left the house, the cow was found dead. Rabbi Joseph was astounded at what Elijah had done, how he had repaid their hosts. But he remembered the condition for the trip, and said nothing.

The next night they stopped at the house of a rich man who did not even offer them food and drink. He kept

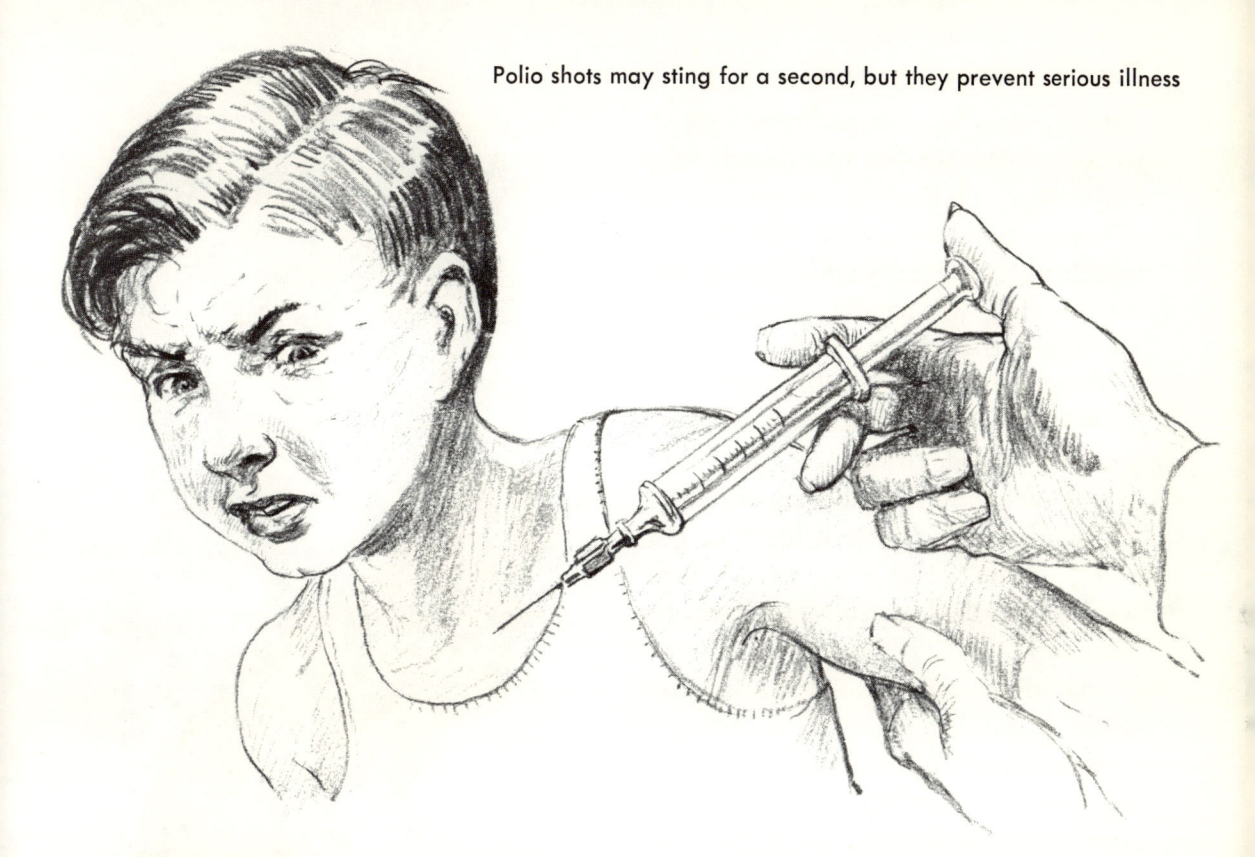

Polio shots may sting for a second, but they prevent serious illness

talking about a wall that had tumbled down and needed to be rebuilt. Before they left the house of this selfish, inhospitable rich man, Elijah prayed—and the wall stood upright! Still Rabbi Joseph did not dare ask why.

Only at the end of their journey did Elijah explain. "Know," he said, "that under the rich man's wall, there was a treasure. Had I left the wall for him to repair, he would have found the treasure. As for the poor man, his cow was killed because I knew that on the same day the death of his wife had been ordained in heaven. I prayed to God to accept the loss of the poor man's cow instead of his wife."

We cannot always understand

So our Rabbis sought to teach us that we cannot know whether there is injustice in all the troubles we see.

Being only human, there are many things in the world we don't know. But we are constantly striving to understand, and even to control, some of life's troubles. Perhaps before long, we will discover cures for cancer and other diseases. Perhaps man will learn how to control floods and storms, and even war. For Judaism believes that mankind can learn and become better and approach the perfection of God's kingdom.

There are things we can do

Already man has learned many ways to control the smaller troubles of life, and each child can learn them. We can be careful with knives and matches and bicycles and cars. When we are sick, we usually get better, if we follow the doctor's instructions.

When there are troubles that we cannot correct or control, then we must try hard to control our own selves. The blind person cannot help his blindness, but he can learn to get along remarkably well in a dark world. The deaf person can learn to read lips.

Sometimes we make a big trouble out of a small one—"a mountain out of a molehill." Only time can tell us whether the trouble is a great one. An airplane looks huge on the ground, but when once it is in the air, at a distance, it seems small as a bird. Sometimes even big troubles seem small when they too have passed and perhaps forgotten.

We can ask ourselves, "Would I think this was a great trouble if it happened to someone else?" And we can answer it also with an old tale, about a stranger who came to a village and promised the people he would lighten their troubles. He told them all to pack their troubles into a bundle and to bring them to the village square that night. When they all had assembled with their packs of troubles, the stranger told them to hang their packs on a line he had stretched across the square. And then he told them to examine all the bundles and to choose the ones they preferred.

After seeing all other troubles, each one quickly seized his own!

Being able to tell the difference between little troubles and big ones is a sign of being grown up. If dad gets a splinter in his finger, he doesn't howl or make a fuss. He knows it is only a small trouble and easy to get rid of.

Things could be worse

With some of our troubles, we say, "This too is for the best." Suppose a child is knocked over by a car and breaks his arm. He and his parents thank God that he didn't get killed. His arm will mend in time.

One of the most famous stories about things that could be worse is the tale of the poor Jew whose home was so miserable he could stand things no longer. He went to his rabbi, and begged for help. "We are so poor that my wife and I and our six children and my mother-in-law, all live in one hut. We are always in each other's way. We scream and yell at each other all day and night. What shall I do?"

"Do you have a goat?" asked the rabbi, after pondering the case.

"I have a poor skinny goat in the yard, it's true," said the man.

"Take it into the house," said the

rabbi. The poor man was dumbfounded, but he did as the rabbi said. After a few days he came running to the rabbi, weeping bitterly. "Rabbi, I am going out of my mind! Things are much worse than before! The goat is smashing everything in the house, climbing over us at night, eating the clothes off our backs! And it bleats all the time! We can't sleep! What shall I do?"

"Go home," said the rabbi, "and take the goat out of your house. God will help you."

The next day, the man came to the rabbi to thank him. "I did as you said. I took the goat out of the house. Ah, now everything is so quiet, there is plenty of room—life is a pleasure!"

What we have learned so far

Life has its troubles as well as its joys. Sometimes we make our own troubles; other times they are not our fault. Sometimes we can do something about our troubles; other times we can only control ourselves.

Why are there troubles and sufferings in the world? Our sages and wise men, through thousands of years, have tried to find the answers to this question. Sometimes an answer fits and we can understand, but there are times when no answer fits. We may search for an answer ourselves. Until we find it, our faith tells us, "only God knows." And we trust in God that whatever may have happened is only for the better.

QUESTIONS TO THINK ABOUT

1. We say that troubles sometimes help us. Being slaves in Egypt helped Jews to learn the value of freedom. Do you remember any time when trouble helped you?

2. Following the rules of safety helps us to avoid trouble and enjoy things more. For example, we can enjoy honey if we know how to avoid the bee's sting. Can you give other examples of how rules help us to enjoy things at home or at school?

QUESTIONS TO ASK YOUR PARENTS

1. Tell the story of the man who came to the rabbi to complain that he could no longer live in his house because it was so overcrowded. Ask your parents if they know any story or can make one up which has the same idea.

2. Sometimes there is no good answer to explain why troubles come to a person and we say "only God knows why." Can your parents give you an example of this and tell you why we must be satisfied with this answer?

UNIT SIX

What Judaism Teaches Us About Prayer

שְׁמַע

CHAPTER XXIII

We Talk to God through Prayer

Sometimes we feel in tune with the universe. We feel as though the sunshine, the birds, the grass in the fields were telling us of God's joy in life. And something in us answers back. Perhaps we hum or whistle or let out a happy yell.

But sometimes we feel that we are cut off and all alone. We cannot explain ourselves even to those nearest to us, to mother or father or grandfather or anyone. Yet something inside us is speaking. To whom? Perhaps alone in bed at night we say the words silently, inside ourselves, talking our hearts out to God.

And we feel better.

We have prayed. Both ways, in joy and in sadness, we have prayed. The spark of God in ourselves has sought to unite itself with God. Prayer is the way we talk to God.

We pray in order to feel closer to God. We pray so that we won't feel alone. When a person walks in the dark, somehow he feels better if he knows that someone he trusts is near him and can hear him.

We pray because of our need to feel God's nearness.

Sometimes we find words for our prayer in ourselves. But more often we use the poems and words of prayer that have already been written down to help us. Many of these prayers begin by praising the greatness of the Lord, the wondrous works of the Almighty.

People need to pray

Is that because God wants to hear us sing His praises?

It is true that human beings like to hear their praises sung. If you bring home a fine report card and show it to your parents, you expect them to praise you. You are disappointed if they are silent. If they say, "What a fine report card! We're proud of you!" you feel happy. People like to be praised and even need it.

But can this be true of God?

And the answer is no, God does not *need* our praise. It is we who need to praise Him. One of our Jewish writers, Isaac Peretz, wrote a story about a pious tailor and his smart young son, which explains this need in us.

Berel's son has been away to college. He has become a doctor and has just returned to their little village. On Sabbath morning, Berel expects his fine son to come to the synagogue with him to pray. But no, the son does not want to go.

"Are you ashamed to be seen with me?" asks Berel.

"God forbid!" says his son.

"Is it because you are a doctor, and a doctor isn't supposed to pray to God or praise Him?"

"No, it's not that either."

At last the young man explains why he won't go to the synagogue. "Father, imagine you are a rich man —"

"All right, I'll imagine!"

"And opposite your house lives a poor widow, maybe with a lot of children, and she needs help. What would you do?"

"Help her, of course!"

"Would you wait for her to come and beg; would you wait for her to fall weeping at your feet?"

"What on earth for? As long as I know —"

We pray in joy and in sadness

"Well, is God better or worse than you?"

"What a question!"

"Doesn't God Himself know who is poor or sick or weak, and what they need? Does He wait to be asked for help? Does He need to be begged and flattered and praised?" demands the son. "Father, how would you like it if someone were to stand up in front of you and start praising you to your face: 'What a fine tailor! What a wonderful tailor! What an honest tailor!'"

And Berel the father answered, "Such praise would be very silly. But —"

"No buts, father! Do you think God wants you to stand up three times daily and tell Him to His face, 'O God, O wonderful God, creator of heaven and earth.' Doesn't He know it better than you?"

The old man thought for a while, but then his face became bright. "You're right!" he told his clever son. "Absolutely right! God already knows that He is a true God, a wonderful God, the only God, creator of heaven and earth. But still a Jew must pray, mustn't he?"

People need to be guided

That is the secret of prayer. It is *we* who feel the need to praise God and not God who needs the praise. We feel the need to unite with something far greater than ourselves. Most often when we pray it is because we feel we need to be guided. We feel we are not wise enough or strong enough to face the problems before us.

Of course we sometimes use prayer as a way of telling our wishes. We pray for a new bicycle or a piano. We even imagine that if we "pray hard enough," God will do what we want. But we really know that prayer is meant to help us do what God wants. It is to help us find our way.

When a man is lost in a dark forest on a starless night, he trusts to his compass to help him. What is a compass? It is a tiny bit of metal that has been given a magnetic charge. And this tiny bit of metal will always turn to the great source of magnetism, and thus it will point the way for the traveller. The spark of God in us is like a compass to guide us. It always turns to the great source. And our prayer is our way of consulting this guide.

We pray that we will be wise enough and good enough to live in God's way. Even when we pray for something that we ourselves want, we often begin by saying, "May it be Thy will, O Lord our God." For we hope that what we want is what should be rightfully ours, in the way of God.

The Hebrew word for prayer, *tefillah*, comes from a word that means "to judge." Thus, praying means "to judge oneself." And this meaning is the key to prayer in Judaism.

We try to judge ourselves, with God's measure. We pray that we may know and do and receive what is right. We do not, we should not, pray for magical gifts. When we pray, we judge ourselves and try to be better people. But we know how little we are in comparison to God's greatness, so we ask for help and mercy, too. We realize how much God does for us, and we thank Him.

God hears our prayers

Judaism tells us that God hears our prayers. In a prayer, which some Jews recite every day, are the words, "For Thou art a God who listens to prayer and to humble, earnest requests."

When we pray sincerely, we feel better or stronger or braver or more peaceful. It is as though these feelings have come back into us from God, who is the great source.

Sometimes, the answer to our prayer is "no." Often this is because we have prayed for something that really cannot be. At other times, the answer is "no" just as the answer of a parent is "no" if we ask for something that is not really good for us.

Things we cannot pray for

There are things for which we cannot, or should not, pray. It is useless to pray that spilled milk will go back into the glass! It is useless to pray that yesterday will come back and happen all over again. It is useless to

There are things for which we cannot pray

pray that a dead puppy will come back to life.

Though these are useless prayers, there is no harm in them, as long as we know they are only impossible wishes. But there is harm in praying for things that are wrong or will hurt someone else.

For instance, the Rabbis tell us that a man who hears a fire alarm must not pray, "May it be Thy will that the fire is not in my home." For this would be like praying for the fire to be in someone else's house. And besides, the fire already is where it is.

Prayer must be sincere

It is wrong to pray while we keep back something. This is insincere. It does no good to pray, "Forgive me for smearing the windows of the lady next door," while you keep back the thought, "If she scolds me, I'll do it again!"

We cannot say one thing and mean another in prayer. Unless we are really sorry for the wrong things we have done, we cannot expect to be forgiven.

It is wrong to pray "automatically." It is not enough to repeat the words of prayer, while our minds or hearts are somewhere else. There is a Hassidic story about Rabbi Levi Yitzhak who spoke to several worshippers one day, just after everybody finished praying. He shook their hands and said, "Shalom Aleichem! Shalom Aleichem!" greeting each one as though he had returned from far away. When they expressed their surprise, he said, "Why are you surprised? Anyone could see just now that you were far away. You, my friend, were on a vacation, and you, my friend, were in the market place. And when the prayers ended, you all returned from your journeys, so of course I said 'Shalom Aleichem' to you!"

Our prayers are meaningless if they are only words without mind or heart, and if they do not come from a humble spirit.

We pray because we know people are small. We know that we ourselves have small limits and need God's help. Even the human beings who know more than we do and can help us, receive their help from God. The rabbi who advises us is such a person. The doctor who comes to us when we are sick knows that his skill and wisdom also come from God. The singer knows that he could practice eighteen hours a day for a hundred years and never learn to sing unless he had God's gift of a voice and a talent for music. Only when we realize our limits can we pray sincerely. And in order really to be able to pray, we must trust in our prayer and in God's help.

What we have learned so far

Prayer is sometimes called "the Service of the Heart." It must come from the heart as well as the mind. It is the way we express ourselves—our deepest feelings and our highest hopes—to God. Just as talking things over with a good friend makes us feel even closer to that friend, so expressing ourselves to God helps us feel closer to Him. Prayer is like a ladder to heaven. Prayer helps us feel God's nearness.

QUESTIONS TO THINK ABOUT

1. Prayer helps us to talk to God. Why should we use the words of others (when we use the Prayer Book) if we want to talk to God?

2. Sometimes we pray for the wrong things and God must say "no" to these prayers. Can you give any example of such wrong prayers?

QUESTIONS TO ASK YOUR PARENTS

1. Ask your parents to explain the idea that God does not need our praises ("Praise ye the Lord to whom all praise is due") but that we need to praise Him.

2. Judaism tells us that God hears our prayers if we are sincere and if we pray God will tell us to do what is right. Ask your parents why such a prayer will always be answered.

CHAPTER XXIV

We Pray In a Synagogue

When we pray, we try to communicate with God. And when we want to communicate with someone, we must first know where he is. Thus a Hassidic rabbi once asked some of his followers, "Where is the dwelling of God?" They laughed and said, "What a question! Doesn't the Holy One fill all the earth with His glorious presence?" But the rabbi gave his own answer to this question, "The Holy One enters only where He is given room to enter." He meant in our hearts.

We all know that a synagogue is a house of prayer. Yet in our Talmud, this is written: "God says to Israel, 'I bade you pray in the synagogue in your city, but if you cannot pray there, pray in your field. And if you cannot pray there, pray on your bed. And if you cannot pray there, then meditate in your heart.'"

Worship in ancient times

Each child finds out by himself some of the experiences of all mankind. Each child, at a certain age, has a wish to make a secret hideaway for himself, where he can think his most precious thoughts alone. And so, in the early days of mankind, each man, in seeking to express his religious feelings, would try to find a special stone or cave, or a special place in the woods, where he could feel the presence of God.

When we get a little older, we want to have a clubhouse, with initiations and passwords for our own little group. It was like this in ancient times, too, as mankind developed. Men gathered in groups, usually as tribes. And each group would feel the need to have a special place to worship.

They worshipped mostly with the idea of winning the favor of their gods. They brought their fruits and grains and animals, and placed them on altars for their gods. In return, they asked their gods to give them things. Sometimes they wanted rain and sometimes they wanted victory over their enemies, and so on. They burned incense to put their gods in a good mood and win their favor. Some ancient people even sacrificed human beings.

The sacrifices were brought to the special place where they believed they made contact with their gods. They believed this could be done only in certain magical places, and sometimes only in one place. And they believed that only certain people could offer the sacrifices, certain people who knew special rites and special words. They must be priests.

How the ancient Hebrews worshipped

The ancient Hebrews began with the same sort of customs. They too burned incense and brought fruits and grains and animals to their tribal altars. We know that Abraham set up such an altar as soon as he came into the Promised Land.

But the Hebrews understood that God did not want human beings to be sacrificed. This is the lesson in the story of Abraham and Isaac. It was a great religious discovery.

We know that some people learn only what they are taught and no more, while others use what they have already learned in order to make new discoveries. That is how the Hebrews differed from the tribes around them. The other tribes did not change their ideas about religion. But the Hebrews kept on discovering more and more about God.

Ancient peoples worshipped in different ways

For a very long time, they too worshipped only in special places. Long after the time of Abraham, long after the time when Moses led them back to the Holy Land, they worshipped on the altar built on Mount Moriah in Jerusalem. This was where they built their Temple.

And only the priests, called Kohanim, and their helpers, called Levites, could offer the sacrifices that the people brought to the altar.

But already the Jews understood that a sacrifice was not a magical trade by which they could get God to do what they wanted. Already they knew that the sacrifice was simply a thankful offering on their own part, a sign of their love and honor to God.

With the sacrifices, the Temple service in ancient times called for the chanting of hymns in praise and thanks to God. Some of the beautiful poems, called Psalms, in the Bible, were among the very ones recited at that time.

And in the service, then as today, they repeated the Sh'ma, which was the first great religious discovery of Judaism:

"Hear, O Israel, the Lord our God, the Lord is One."

While the people all around them were still worshipping many gods, our people had discovered there is only one God. While the people around them were still sacrificing human beings, our people had learned this is wrong. Yet they still believed that the worship of God had to be done in only one certain place—in the Temple in Jerusalem. From all over Palestine, they came for the services to Jerusalem. And they still believed that only the priests could offer the people's sacrifices to God.

How the synagogue began

And then a dreadful thing happened —and they learned from it.

The Temple was destroyed. More than twenty-five hundred years ago,

Worshippers came to the Temple from all over the Holy Land

invaders came and conquered Jerusalem, burned and wrecked the Temple, and took the Jews as captives to Babylonia.

They no longer had their Temple at which to worship. Priests could no longer offer sacrifices. But they realized that they still had their religion. They carried Judaism in their hearts and minds.

They made their next great discovery—that God need not be worshipped in one solitary place, but that God could be worshipped everywhere. Though they did not have their Temple at which to bring sacrifice, they still had the laws of God given to Moses. They gathered together to discuss these laws, and appointed scribes to write them down. Wherever they were, they could study the Torah and praise God.

These gatherings became the first synagogues. The word "synagogue"

159

CHINA

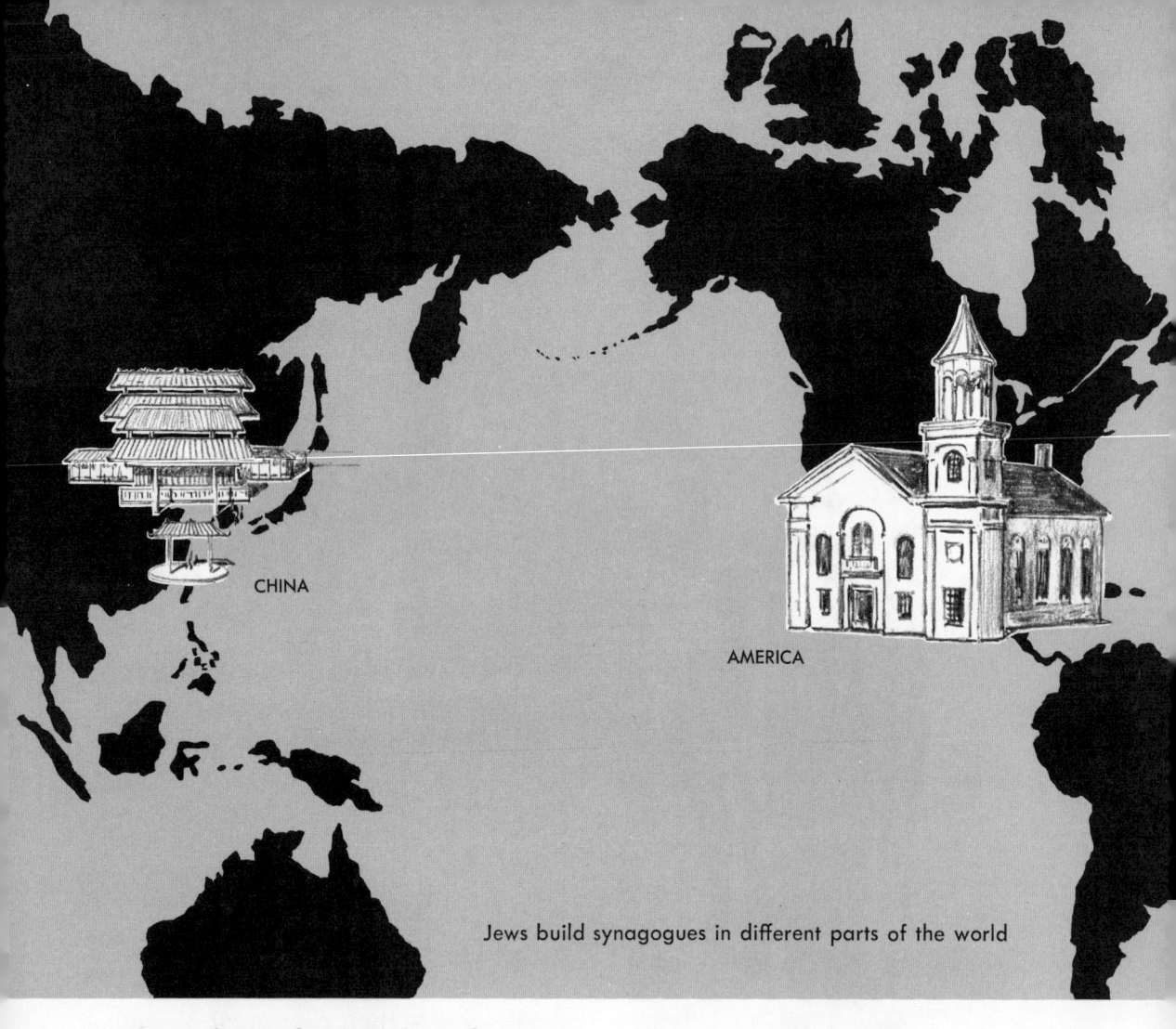

AMERICA

Jews build synagogues in different parts of the world

comes from the Greek and means "gathering together." It is a translation of the Hebrew name, *Beth Knesseth,* which means "house of gathering."

When they returned to Jerusalem, the Jews built the Second Temple and restored their custom of the Temple sacrifice. But they also brought back with them their newer custom of gathering together for prayer and study. So they came to have a *Beth Knesseth,* or synagogue, in their towns and villages, as well as the Temple for the great services in Jerusalem.

And when the Temple was destroyed a second time, the sacrifices again stopped, but the meetings in the synagogues continued. Wherever the Jews were driven, in each city and each country to which their wanderings took them, they carried God's laws in their Torah, and they built their synagogues.

Now, other religions began to understand the great discovery of

160

Judaism. Instead of many gods, each with his sacred place of worship, there was only one God, who could be worshipped everywhere.

Two new religions arose, the Christian and the Mohammedan religion, and their churches and mosques began as copies of the synagogue.

Prayer became the way of worship

Prayer, which is the "service of the heart," took the place of sacrifice as a way of worship. Prayer need not be limited to a single place, such as the Temple in Jerusalem.

It is the purpose for which people gather that really makes the place holy. The place by itself has no "magic." It is not holy by itself.

Our prayers are divided into personal prayers and group prayers, often called services. Services may be held in any clean place where Jews gather to pray.

We no longer have priests to lead the services, for a rabbi is not the same as a priest. The title "rabbi" simply means "my teacher." The rabbi has learned more about our Torah and about Judaism than most of us. He devotes his life to this learning and to helping others to understand. Usually the rabbi leads us in our services, but it is not this that makes him the rabbi. Any Jew who knows how may lead the services. Any group of ten or more Jews may hold a service; it is not necessary for a rabbi to be present. The rabbi is most important to us for his learning, and thus we see that learning itself became a very important part of Judaism.

Synagogues remind us of the Temple

Every synagogue tries in some ways to remind us of the Temple in Jerusalem. Synagogues all over the world are built so that the worshippers face toward Jerusalem. In America, they face eastward because Jerusalem is east of us. In Yemen they face toward the north. In India they face toward the west. In Israel itself, they face toward Jerusalem. And in Jerusalem, they face toward Mount Moriah, where the ancient Temple used to stand.

Why do we have public prayers?

Since everyone may pray by himself, at any time or place, in his own words or in regular prayers, why do we have public prayers? Simply because people like to do things together with other people. We like to live near other people, not always alone in the woods. We like the feeling of belonging to a group. We enjoy parties because we like to share our fun with other people. We like to pray together with other people because much of what we pray for in the world concerns other people, too.

Judaism has always taught us that the well-being of the group is important, just as is the well-being of each person. When we pray together in a group, our prayers are less likely to be selfish and petty.

What we have learned so far

It is a beautiful feeling to enter a synagogue and know that we are praying in the same kind of place and in the same way as other Jews, all over the world and all through the ages. We can pray in a synagogue in Rome or in Paris or in Africa, and feel at home. The synagogue and the familiar prayers help tie us all together. They help us feel closer to the people with whom we pray. And they help us feel closer to God.

QUESTIONS TO THINK ABOUT

1. Although Jews may pray anywhere, they have always had special places where they came together to pray. Do you remember the places where prayers were recited by Abraham, by Moses and by Solomon?

2. What does "Beth Knesseth," the Hebrew word used for synagogue, mean if we translate it exactly? What does it tell us about the synagogue?

QUESTIONS TO ASK YOUR PARENTS

1. One reason for praying in public is that we are more likely to pray for the welfare of others instead of thinking only of ourselves. Ask your parents why this is important in Judaism.

2. Jews can feel at home in synagogues anywhere in the world. Ask your parents if they have ever visited a synagogue in another city or another country and how they felt when they took part in the services there.

CHAPTER XXV

A Prayer Book Helps Us to Pray

When our prayer is personal, we may pray at home, at school, in the synagogue, in the car, or anywhere. We may pray in our own words, or in poems from the Bible, or in words from other books, or in no words at all. For it is our feeling of need that makes us pray.

Sometimes we forget that when we pray in a public service at the synagogue, using the prayers that have been written out for us, our feelings are just as important as the words.

A shepherd boy prays

A tale is told of the rabbi called the Baal Shem Tov. One day he was about to enter the synagogue in his little town of Medzibuz, but he drew back from the door. "I cannot go in there," he said. "There is no room for me!"

His followers, the Hassidim, said, "But the synagogue isn't full!"

"The house is filled from the ground to the roof with prayers," said the Baal Shem Tov. And as he saw the Hassidim taking pride in his words, he said, "Those prayers are all dead prayers. They have no strength to fly to heaven. The synagogue is filled with them!"

Now near Medzibuz there lived a Jewish herdsman. This man had an only son, who was so slow-witted that he could not remember the alphabet. But as his thirteenth birthday approached, the father brought him to the synagogue, to try at least to teach him how to pray. They arrived just then.

As the Baal Shem Tov saw them entering the synagogue, he suddenly went in after them, followed by his Hassidim. All through the evening service, the Baal Shem prayed with fervor, trying to force the prayers up to heaven. But even the Baal Shem's prayers fell back.

The shepherd boy sat silently beside his father, staring at the Prayer Book which had been put into his hands.

Then came the time when all arose

for the great prayer called "the Amidah," the standing prayer, which is spoken by the lips but in silence. The shepherd boy arose, too.

The outspread hands of the Baal Shem were raised in supplication.

Suddenly, through the silent synagogue, there came the sound of a shepherd's flute.

The worshippers turned to the boy in horror. They looked as if they expected the walls to fall in on them. But a flood of joy came over the face of the Baal Shem Tov. He knew that the flute was the shepherd boy's way of praying to God. "The prayers are on their way!" cried the Baal Shem Tov. "All our dead prayers are stirring, and rising to heaven!" And he came to the boy, and put his hands on his head, and blessed him.

Why we need a Prayer Book

The very word, "Hassid" means pious. There are many such Hassidic stories which tell us that the feeling of a prayer is more important than the words. Nevertheless, there are times when we want to pray, and we don't exactly know how. Then the words of an ancient prayer can help us. They seem to show us what we really mean. And because we know that these same words have been spoken through so many centuries by so many of our people who had the same feelings, we are comforted. It is as though the whole great chorus of the past were giving strength to our prayers.

If we prayed only in our own words, and only when we "felt like it," we would be more likely to pray only to ask for personal things. When children go to camp, their letters home are often lists of "please send me." Many grownups are like children. They turn to prayer only when they want something.

Our written prayers and our regular services help us to turn to God about other things, as well as about our personal needs.

When we want to thank God about important things, or turn to God about important problems, we often feel we cannot find the right words. Greater minds and greater souls than ours have given us words in these prayers, and often, as we repeat them, something inside us says, "Yes, yes, that's exactly what I wanted to say!"

Every child knows this, from birthdays, and other times when mother or dad says, "You must write a thank-you note." And the child puts it off, and puzzles, and finally, sitting in front of the writing paper, begs, "What shall I say!"

The Prayer Book unites all Jews

Our book of prayers not only helps us in what to say, but it brings us together with other Jews in our prayers. If a group of Jews tried praying, each in his own words, then each of them would probably be praying only for himself and his own family, instead of for the community and the world as well. And they would be out of harmony, like a number of people singing different songs at the same time.

With the Prayer Book, we pray together for things that are important to the Jews and to all people, not just to ourselves alone. Our prayers were chosen through the ages, so that only the most meaningful were kept. Our wisest and holiest men chose the prayers for the services.

We always turn to people of experience for the best. Most families have a camera and take snapshots. But when they want a really fine picture, they go to a photographer, who will see that the lighting is good and that nothing important is left out. In the same way, for prayers written by experts, we turn to our book of prayers.

Why we pray in Hebrew

Why does our Prayer Book use Hebrew instead of only English, which we understand so much better? He-

Hebrew prayer makes us feel united with Jews all over the world

brew connects us with all the Jews, past and present, all over the world.

Our Bible was written in Hebrew, and because our Bible is our Holy Book, Hebrew became our Holy Language. Even when the Jews were scattered in many countries and spoke the languages of the countries where they lived, they kept Hebrew as their language for holy purposes, for praying.

As time went by, masses of Jews did not have the time or the means to learn Hebrew well. So, in order to participate in public praying, they learned to read the sounds of the words, by learning the alphabet, even though they did not always know the meaning. They felt, perhaps like the boy with the flute, that their hearts were in the sounds, and that the sound of Hebrew was holy in itself.

Today we have translations in our Prayer Book, for those who don't understand Hebrew. We can pray in any language, and we often mingle Hebrew prayers with prayers in English, because we too feel that the sound of Hebrew is a symbol of prayer.

Of course, we want to learn Hebrew well enough so that we know the meaning of each word as we speak it. We want to learn Hebrew, also, so that if we visit Israel we can speak with the people in the old-new tongue of our people. But even if we only know how to read the sounds, Hebrew makes us feel united with Jews all over the world.

Even by only knowing the sounds, a Jew from France and from Yemen and from America can pray together, though they might not be able to talk together.

Hebrew puts us into a special mood for prayer, just because we know it is and has always been the language of our prayer.

167

David, the shepherd boy, composed many of the psalms we now use in prayer

The prayers in our service

The Hebrew name of our Prayer Book is Siddur, which means the "arrangement," or the "order." We have many different kinds of Prayer Books. There is the Ashkenazic one used by most American and European Jews, the Sephardic one which the descendants of Spanish and Portuguese Jews pray from; the Yemenite one, used by those Jews who were for centuries isolated in that distant South Arabian kingdom. And many other varieties of Siddur too.

But if because we Jews were scattered around the world, we had differing versions of the Prayer Book, they were all built around the same basic Siddur. Sometimes, in one place, we choose one psalm or prayer or poem, and in another place another psalm or prayer or poem.

In America and England, where there are many Conservative and Reform Jews, there are Prayer Books which have been developed from the traditional Siddur. They are shorter, yet their order is the same. The Bar'chu, the Sh'ma and the Kaddish, as well as many other prayers are there. Some prayers have been shortened, a few eliminated, and there are some new ones that have been introduced.

Most important is the Sh'ma. This is our declaration of faith:

"Hear, O Israel, the Lord our God, the Lord is One."

All of Judaism depends on this first great truth, that there is One God.

Before and after the Sh'ma, there are psalms and blessings praising and thanking God. Then in the traditional service, there comes the time of the standing prayer, the Amidah, also called Sh'moneh Esreh.

At the end of the service comes the Alenu, a prayer that was written for the Holy Days, but our ancestors added it later to our every day prayers. During every service, the "Kaddish," our hymn to the holiness of God, is recited.

The Prayer Book has many additions that may be used for the prayer services. And besides the daily or Sabbath Prayer Book, there are special holiday Prayer Books, which give us the respective prayers and hymns for the Holy Days and the Festivals.

What we have learned so far

Our Prayer Books are collections of prayers carefully made throughout the ages. Although we may pray by ourselves in any words we choose, the words of the old prayers are sometimes just what we want to say. Many prayers are quotations from the Bible. At different times in our prayers we repeat the great hymns and psalms. There are also prayers that were written in different centuries, in different parts of the world, and that were added to the services because they were so good. The Prayer Book is a treasure house of Judaism. It helps us feel that Jews have always felt close to God, and that God is close to us.

QUESTIONS TO THINK ABOUT

1. How does the story of Baal Shem Tov and the shepherd boy's flute tell us that feelings are sometimes more important than words in offering prayers?

2. Hebrew prayers unite Jews all over the world because they are recited in every synagogue no matter what the language of the land may be. What other reasons are given in this chapter for learning our prayers in Hebrew?

QUESTIONS TO ASK YOUR PARENTS

1. Just as we respect the work of experts in any field, we choose many of our prayers from the Psalms in the Bible and from the work of the great Hebrew poets of later times. Ask your parents why so many of the most famous prayers are Psalms.

2. Many families own Prayer Books which once belonged to grandparents or great-grandparents. Ask your parents if they have Prayer Books like this or if they remember seeing them in their parents' homes.

CHAPTER XXVI

There Are Times to Pray

Since we can pray at any time we feel like praying, why are there special times for prayer? And the answer is, that we shall remember to pray.

We all know how we put off things we can "always do." If mother says, "Stop in and get a haircut whenever you can," you may forget about it or put it off for weeks. But if she says, "You have an appointment for a haircut at four o'clock," you will go there.

Why we have set services

Many Jews pray regularly every day, without having to be reminded. And every Jew should know the ways of prayer, so that he can use them when he wishes to pray or has need to pray.

There are set services for every day—in the morning, in the afternoon before sunset, and again at night after the sun goes down. There are set services for the Sabbath, with special prayers to welcome it and special prayers and ceremonies to take leave from it. There are set services for all the holidays with special prayers for each occasion.

We have set prayers for the great moments in our lives

Then we have prayers and ceremonies for the important times in our own lives. On the eighth day after a boy is born, there is a ceremony called a B'rith, which is a way of saying that the boy is part of the Jewish people.

At the age of thirteen, a boy becomes Bar Mitzvah, and a girl becomes Bat Mitzvah. They then become responsible for behaving as good Jews should.

When people marry, there is a special marriage ceremony which asks God's blessing on the bride and groom and thanks Him for the joy of a happy couple.

And just as we have prayers and ceremonies for happy times, so we have prayers when there is the sorrow of death. In sad times and in happy times, we praise God.

So Jewish tradition has prepared for us a constant and continuous way to express our union with God. On each day, on each Sabbath, on each holiday, we have our prayers and our ceremonies. And for the great occasions in each person's life, there are special prayers to help us remember that life is holy.

Private prayers

Have you ever felt you were lost and then suddenly you heard the voices of your parents, looking for you, calling to you? Then perhaps you felt like whispering, "Thank you, God!" If you did, that was a prayer, and a prayer of the purest kind.

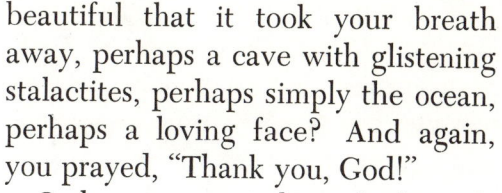

Have you ever seen something so beautiful that it took your breath away, perhaps a cave with glistening stalactites, perhaps simply the ocean, perhaps a loving face? And again, you prayed, "Thank you, God!"

Or have you ever been frightened, and thought, "Please help me, God!" You most likely knew you were praying then.

We often pray alone, expressing joy or fear

171

We pray each time we express our joys, our fears, our feelings to God. Many times we feel like praying in our own words, all by ourselves. And other times we want to pray, either alone or with our families, using words that belong to a set prayer, to tradition.

Before sleeping, we sometimes have this feeling. And so, by tradition, we repeat the great avowal of our faith, the Sh'ma, as we go to bed. On waking, we may want to thank God in our own words, or in words of the Prayer Book, for a new day.

Blessings are a way of thanking God

All through the day there are moments when we can make a little ceremony for ourselves, if we want to. In the past, when Jewish life was much more ceremonial, one could hear blessings for almost every little act of life.

When a pious Jew took a drink, he said a blessing; when he cut a piece of bread, he said a blessing. Perhaps we wonder, why there were so many blessings. But don't we have manners of our own that are very similar? When we ask someone to pass the salt, we say "please" and "thank you." When we ask for a drink of water or a slice of bread, we say "please" and "thank you." The pious Jews were only saying the same "thank you" to God.

This is called a "b'rachah." A b'rachah, or blessing, is a short prayer which praises or thanks God for a particular gift. There are quite a few such blessings, and many of them are familiar to us all.

A b'rachah begins with the Hebrew words, *Baruch Attah*—"Blessed art Thou, O Lord our God, King of the Universe."

Blessings for food

Naturally, many of our blessings come at mealtimes. Almost everyone feels grateful to God for providing the food that keeps us alive. And many families keep up the custom of having a blessing when they sit down at the table and a blessing when they rise.

We thank God for the food which He provides. The blessing we use most often is the one when "bread is broken."

Blessed art Thou, O Lord our God, King of the Universe, who bringest forth bread from the earth.

For fruit, the last words are *who createst the fruit of the tree.* For wine we say, *who createst the fruit of the vine.* For some other foods, we simply say, *who createst various kinds of food.*

Other kinds of blessings

In the Siddur we can find a whole list of blessings—blessings on seeing lightning, on seeing falling stars, on hearing thunder, on beholding the great sea or a rainbow or the first blossoms of spring. Surely this is like our own impulse to say "Thank you, God," on seeing nature's wonders.

In our daily lives, we have blessings, already written, that meet every imaginable event. There are blessings for coming into a brand new house, or a new land. There are blessings for escape from a shipwreck, for being healed from sickness, for escape from all kinds of danger. And there is a general blessing, for being alive, which is used on many occasions. It is called the *Shehecheyanu.*

Blessed art Thou, O Lord our God, King of the universe, who hast kept us in life, and hast preserved us, and hast enabled us to reach this season.

A blessing for escape from danger

During the Second World War, on December 13, 1940, a Friday evening, bombs fell on an English city, killing hundreds of people. Many Jews were among them.

In the synagogue on the next morning, which was the Sabbath, the survivors stood up, all of them in tears, repeating the special b'rachah of those who have escaped great peril:

Blessed art Thou, O Lord our God, King of the Universe, who doest good to the undeserving and who hast dealt kindly with me.

Blessing over the Sabbath and holiday candles

We have special blessings for the lighting of candles on Sabbath and holidays. For Sabbath, mother says: *Blessed art Thou, O Lord our God, King of the Universe, who hast sanctified us by Thy commandments and commanded us to kindle the Sabbath lights.*

For each of the holidays, we have blessings. On Passover we have many blessings at the Seder. On Hanukah we bless the candles for eight nights.

Some famous prayers

All these set prayers are ready for us, to help us express our faith. In old times, many rabbis created their own private prayers, which were then used by their followers. The great sage Rav had a favorite prayer:

May it be Thy will, O Lord our God, to grant us long life, a life of peace, a life of good, a life of blessing, a life of sustenance, a life of bodily vigor, a life marked by the fear of sin, a life free of shame and reproach, a life of prosperity and honor, a life in which the love of the Torah and the fear of heaven shall cling to us, a life wherein Thou fulfillest the desires of the heart for good.

Another famous rabbi, Hiya bar Abba, had a short prayer which reminds us of Hillel:

Let our hearts be united in fear of Thy name; bring us near to what Thou lovest; keep us far from what Thou hatest.

Our private prayers

Each of us can have his own private prayers, in his own words. On a birthday or a graduation day, we may prefer to use our own words to thank God for the joy and pleasure of that day. When we are sick or someone we love is sick, we may find our own prayers for health. When we have done something wrong, like lying or stealing, we can pray and tell God in our own way that we are sorry for the wrong things we did, and ask Him to help us to become better people.

What we have learned so far

In the lives of every one of us, there are everyday things that happen over and over and yet are new and miraculous each time. For each of these experiences, Judaism has provided us with words to express our wonder and our thanks. Yet each life is different from any other, and so each of us at times finds words of his own, ways of his own, times of his own, to tell God his thanks, to ask for God's help, to pray.

QUESTIONS TO THINK ABOUT

1. Why is it important to have a set time for prayer instead of waiting until you feel like praying? Can you give an example of how you put off something important because it didn't have to be done at a certain time?

2. Blessings are a way of thanking God. Do you remember the reasons for thanking God in the blessings mentioned in this chapter?

QUESTIONS TO ASK YOUR PARENTS

1. There are also times when Jews are asked to make up their own prayers. Ask your parents when would be a good time for your family to recite a prayer written by someone in the family.

2. Jews have prayer services for each day, for the Sabbath and holy days, and for every important event in a person's lifetime. Ask your parents why prayer is so important in living as a Jew.

CHAPTER XXVII

There Are Many Kinds of Prayer

When we pray to God in our own way, about our own problems, about our own doubts, and when we thank God for our very own happiness, we speak the language of "I" and "Thou." We speak from ourselves to Him in a very personal way. Sometimes we whisper secrets that are very personal. There might be feelings of shame, or joy, so personal that we can't tell them to anyone but God. So we say "I."

But when we speak to God through our regular prayers, we say "we." Why don't we still say "I"? Of course each of us is inside the "we," and strangely enough, very often we forget that we are using the plural, and "we" seems "I." It seems that we count for everyone, and everyone counts for us.

For instance, in our daily prayers we confess that we have sinned and ask God's pardon. In the Amidah, the traditional Jew says:

Forgive us, our Father, for we have sinned; pardon us, O King, for we have transgressed; for Thou dost pardon and forgive. Blessed art Thou, O Lord, who art gracious, and dost abundantly forgive.

We are part of a group

We are praying not only because of our own mistakes and wrongdoings, but for all humanity together.

On Yom Kippur, there is a long list of sins in the traditional prayers, for which we all ask to be forgiven. None of us really has broken the whole list! Yet each of us feels a little bit as though he had committed every sin on that list because he knows that it has been done. You, yourself, may only have lied a little bit during the year, maybe only small lies, and you may not even have stolen so much as a package of gum out of the supermarket, but when you read the list and it says, "we have lied, we have stolen, we have said bad things about other people," you feel that you are indeed part of it. We confess the sins of all human beings, because we remember that we are part of a larger group, of all people. In the same way, we speak for all people when we ask God for help, and we know that they speak for each of us.

We ask God for important things

Here are some of the things asked for in the Amidah each day, over and over, because people are never done needing them:

We pray to God to give us understanding and wisdom.

We pray that He will help us repent for any wrong we have done.

We pray that He will forgive us.

We pray that He will keep us from trouble and will help us when we are in trouble.

We pray that He will heal us from sickness.

We pray that He will give us the things we need to live.

In each of these prayers, what we ask for is personal—each person feels he is asking for understanding, forgiveness and health for his own self. But even when he speaks this prayer alone at home, rather than in the synagogue, he says "we." He says "help us." For in Judaism we try never to forget that we are part of humanity.

We pray as part of a group

We do not ask for riches and power. The great Hebrew poet, Bialik, reminds us that Jews in all ages put wisdom above wealth. "If God had appeared to our pious mothers, and said to them, as He did to Solomon of old, 'Ask, what shall I give thee?' they would have answered, 'I ask for no riches or honors for myself; but O, may it be Thy will, Lord of the universe, that Thou givest my children an understanding heart in Torah and wisdom, so as to discern the eternal difference between good and evil.'"

We ask for wisdom in our prayers.

We remember our people's past

And in our prayers, we remind ourselves of our Jewish past, and we speak of the hopes for our people.

Again and again in our prayers, we remind ourselves that God freed us from slavery in Egypt. This is repeated in the Kiddush and in many, many prayers. On Passover, at the Seder, we say that each one of us should feel as though he, personally, had been freed from slavery in Egypt.

In this way we strongly tell ourselves that each person has the whole past and future of his people and of the world within him. He is part of all.

We remind ourselves in other prayers of how God saved our people. On Hanukah and on Purim we recall such great events. And each day in our prayers we remind ourselves that our people are scattered over the earth.

We pray for the future of our people

Many Jews pray that they be gathered together once more into the land from which the Jews were scattered. Already this prayer, repeated over the centuries, is coming true. Jews from all over the world are gathering together in the State of Israel. All who wish to live there are welcomed. They come from many lands where they have been oppressed, and some come

Many Jews pray that our people be gathered once more into the land from which they were scattered

from lands of freedom, like our own, simply because they wish to live in Israel.

But there are still other lands, from which Jews are not allowed to leave; and so we pray that all Jews who wish to return and live in Israel may be free to do so.

Many Jews pray for Jerusalem, the Holy City. We pray that God will help our people in the future as He has helped us in the past. In all such prayers, the "we" becomes indeed a prayer for the group, more than for our own personal selves.

We pray for the people of the world

So our prayers go beyond ourselves to our people and to all humanity. We pray that God will help the nations of the world live together in peace.

In the Alenu, we pray that all people will understand that there is One God in all the world and that they will be united under the Kingship of God. The Siddur says:

. . . when the world will be perfected under the Kingdom of the Almighty, and all people will call upon Thy name.

We thank God for His daily wonders

But prayer is not only for asking. We also give thanks. Just as each of us alone often says a silent "Thank you, God" for the beauty and goodness of the world, so in our prayer, called *Modim Anachnu*, we end with a "Thank you, God." We pray:

> *We will give thanks to Thee and declare Thy praise for our lives which are committed unto Thy hand, and for our souls, which are in Thy charge, and for Thy miracles, which are daily with us, and for Thy wonders and Thy benefits, which are wrought at all times, evening, morn, and noon...*

And in another prayer we say:

> *Who is like unto Thee, O Lord, among the mighty? Who is like unto Thee, glorious in holiness, revered in praises, doing marvels?*

One of our most beautiful prayers of thanks is said on Sabbaths and festivals:

> *Were our mouth full of song as the sea, and our tongue of exultation as the multitude of its waves, and our lips of praise as its wide-extended skies; were our eyes shining with light as the sun and the moon, and our hands were spread forth as the eagles of the air, and our feet were swift as the wild deer, we should still be unable to thank Thee and to bless Thy name, O Lord our God and God of our fathers, for one thousandth or one ten-thousandth part of the bounties which Thou hast bestowed upon our fathers and upon us.*

So in our prayers together we thank God for all that we have been, that we are, and that we want to be. We ask for understanding, so that we can make ourselves better and the world better.

The familiar hymn, "Adon Olam," too, reminds us that there is only One God. But it does more. It reminds us that we are always in His care, that we can trust Him. It is an expression of our faith in God.

What we have learned so far

We pray to express our faith in God and to give thanks to Him. Sometimes we pray only for ourselves and so we say "I." But we also pray for all other Jews and for all people in the world. And that is why, in most of our prayers, we say "we." Each of us is included in the "we" of our prayers. We all share in God's love.

QUESTIONS TO THINK ABOUT

1. Why do some of our most important prayers begin with "we," especially when worshippers ask for forgiveness from sins?

2. Many prayers remind us of events in the long history of the Jewish people. Which events are recalled in the prayers on Passover, on Shavuoth, on Sukkoth, on Hanukah and on Purim?

QUESTIONS TO ASK YOUR PARENTS

1. In many prayers, Jews ask for wisdom and understanding instead of for wealth. Ask your parents why Jews consider wisdom so important.

2. Jews also pray for the future of all Jews and for the future of all peoples. Why will the world be perfect when all people will be united in the worshipping of One God?

CHAPTER XXVIII

Study Is Part of Prayer

Have you ever tried to keep tiny fish in a tank? If you want them to live, you must learn more and more about them. You must know the exact right temperature for their water, and how to keep the water clean, and what to feed them and how much and when. Soon you want to learn the names of the different kinds of tiny fish moving like jewels in the water. You want to know the habits of each kind, so as to help it live and breed.

If you don't know about fish, you quickly lose interest, and soon lose the fish, too.

So the Jews knew long ago, that if they did not study Judaism, they would soon cease to be Jews. It was the law of God in their Torah, that held their life. The Torah has often been compared to a sea, and a bright scholar to one who swims freely in its waters. And there is even a story about Rabbi Akiba, which tells us that a Jew without study of Judaism is just like a fish out of the water.

Rabbi Akiba lived in Palestine after the Romans had already destroyed the Temple in Jerusalem. The Jews left in Palestine had tried to keep Judaism alive by slipping away to small villages, where they started schools of the Torah. But the Romans found out about this and soon forbade these studies.

Rabbi Akiba gathered his students and moved to a cave. An old friend of his, Pappos ben Judah, came to visit him one day. Pappos wanted to save Akiba, so he reminded him of the terrible power of the Romans. "Suppose they find you! Aren't you afraid?"

"I will answer you," said Rabbi Akiba. "My students and I are like fish in a stream who gather together and move from one place to another. If a fox came along the bank of the river, and asked, 'From what are you fleeing?' They would answer, 'From the nets, which are set to catch us.' If then the fox said, 'Come up to dry land, my dear fishes, and we shall dwell together, just as my fathers dwelt with your fathers.' Then the fish would reply 'Are you the one, of whom they say that he is the cleverest of animals? You are not so clever, if you think that we are so foolish! For if we are afraid to stay in the water which is our life element, how much more afraid should we be to leave it and go out where we surely cannot live!'"

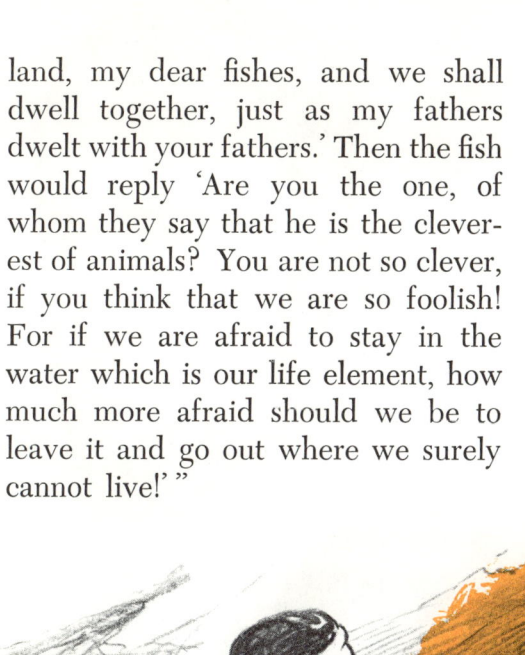

"So it is with us," Rabbi Akiba added. "It is written about the Torah, 'It is thy life and the length of thy days.' If we are in danger even now while we sit and study the Torah, how much greater will be our danger if we leave our life-giving studies?"

Moses Maimonides, medicine and philosophy

Heinrich Hertz, physics

Baruch Spinoza, philosophy

Study is God's way

But Jews did not study the Torah for the sake of study alone. Jews studied the Torah so that they might learn God's will, and be able *to do it*.

We know the story of Hillel, who taught the Torah before the days of Rabbi Akiba. We know how a man came to Hillel and asked to be taught the Torah while he stood on one foot, and Hillel told him the rule, "Do not do to your fellow man what you hate to have done unto you." But what Hillel added is just as important. "That is the whole Torah," Hillel said, "the rest is commentary. *Now go, and study.*"

There is another story about Hillel, and his great debate with Rabbi Tarfon and the elders of the community. The question was raised, "Is study greater, or doing?" Rabbi Tarfon said, "Doing is greater!" But Hillel said, "Study is greater, for it leads to

Paul Ehrlich, medicine

Sigmund Freud, psychoanalysis

Albert Einstein, physics and mathematics

Louis Brandeis, law

doing." And everyone else agreed.

Our people have always honored the scholar above all others. And though not everyone could become a scholar, each Jew has always been urged to learn as much as he could. In ancient times when even kings did not know how to sign their names, ordinary Jews learned to read and write—at least to read enough so that they could say their prayers.

From the oldest times, a scholar has been a prize in a family, and rich men have sought for the brightest scholars to marry their daughters. For a scholar was "the jewel in the family crown."

The custom of seeking a great scholar for a son-in-law gave rise to many stories, all the way into modern times. There are many stories about wealthy Jews who sent scouts to all the great Talmud academies, to seek the brightest students as husbands for their daughters. It is always the poorest young man in these stories, who is the most brilliant.

Study is for everyone

But while we praise and reward our brightest students, we have schools for everyone. The learning of God is for everyone. For each of us must learn, in order to be able to *do it*.

In the Bible, right after we are given the words of the Sh'ma, Hear O Israel, we are told, "And thou shalt love the Lord thy God with all thy heart, and with all thy soul, and with all thy might. And these words which I command thee this day, shall be upon thy heart, and thou shalt *teach* them diligently unto thy children."

Pious Jews repeat this prayer every day. It is a vow to learn and to teach. Again and again in the Amidah, the very first thing a Jew asks of God is knowledge:

Thou favorest man with knowledge, and teachest mortals understanding. O favor us with knowledge, understanding and discernment from Thee. Blessed art Thou, O Lord, gracious Giver of knowledge.

This is knowledge of the "laws of life" for each of us, for everyone, so that we may learn and teach and do God's will.

"As water is free to all, so is the Torah free to all," said our Rabbis of old. "As water is priceless, so is the Torah priceless. As water brings life to the world, so the Torah brings life to the world. As water brings a man out of his uncleanness, so the Torah brings a man from the evil way into the good way."

The study of Torah is the best crown

The Rabbis also told us that the study of God's Law, which is open to all, is the highest crown of all, so that each man may sit with the highest.

There are three crowns, we are told—the crown of the Torah, the crown of Priesthood, and the crown of the Kingdom. Aaron was worthy of the crown of Priesthood, and got it. David was worthy of the crown of the Kingdom, and got it. But the crown of the Torah, we are told, remains for everyone who will wear it. It is kept for everyone. For God says, "Of him who proves himself worthy of *that* crown, I reckon it as if he had proved himself worthy of them all!"

What we have learned so far

Learning is never ended. In Judaism, we continue to discover wisdom that has not been understood before. The rabbis of old said, "When God revealed His presence to the Israelites, He did not show forth all His goodness at once, because they could not have borne so much good!"

Each Jew seeks all his life to discover all that he can of God's goodness. And so, as this little beginning of learning is ended, remember the words of Hillel: "Go now, and study!"

QUESTIONS TO THINK ABOUT

1. How does the Rabbi Akiba story of the "Fox and the Fish" tell us that study of the Torah is most important?

2. Some people remember only the first part of the story in which Hillel is asked to be taught the Torah while he stood on one foot. Hillel ends the story by saying "Now go, and study." Why is this as important as the first part of Hillel's answer?

QUESTIONS TO ASK YOUR PARENTS

1. In the past Jews always hoped to have a scholar in the family. Sons who were very bright were sent to the best schools to study. Parents who had a daughter tried to arrange a marriage with a bright student, even if the daughter's family was very wealthy and the students' family was very poor. Is this still true today?

2. The Rabbis taught the "crown of Torah" can be worn by anyone who earns it by studying. How can parents earn the "crown of Torah" in our own synagogues?

TEACHER AND DISCIPLES

HOUSE OF STUDY

CHEDER

How Jews have studied through the centuries

MODERN SEMINARY

Index

Abel, 85, 121
Abraham, 17-22, 26, 27, 29, 57-58, 133-134, 157
Abraham, the first Jew, 20
Adam, 20, 78-79, 98, 106, 140-142
Adamah, 106
Adonai, 68
Adon Olam, 180
Akiba, 72, 124, 182-183
Alenu, 169, 179
America, 20, 55, 72, 100, 162, 167, 168
Amidah, 169, 176-177, 186
Arab, 138
Archeology, 17
Ashkenazic, 168
Atonement, Day of, 120

Baal Shem Tov, 132, 164-165
Babylon, 81
Babylonia, 58-59, 159
Bad Whisper, 72, 74, 76
Bar'chu, 168
Bar Levi, 92
Bar Mitzvah, 170
Bartholomew, 86-87
Baruch Attah, 172
Bat Mitzvah, 170
Beth Knesseth, 160
Bialik, 178
Bible, 20, 30, 45, 50, 57, 58, 61, 63, 78, 79, 80, 89, 98, 104, 106, 112, 120, 122, 124, 128-129, 133, 144, 158, 164, 167, 169, 186
Book of Prayers, 166
B'rachah, 172
B'rith, 170

Cain, 85, 121
Canaan, 20
Charity, 91-93, 97, 99, 139
Children of Israel, 80

Chosen People, 57
Columbus, 73, 100, 103
Conservative Jews, 168
Covenant, 57
Cracow, 134-135
Creation, Story of, 128
Creator, Hand of, 41
"Crown of Creation," 104
Crown of the Kingdom, 186
Crown of Priesthood, 186
Crown of the Torah, 186

David (King), 84, 108
Day of Atonement, 120
Declaration of Faith, 169
Denmark, 102
Dudaleh (Hassidic Song), 132

Eden, Garden of, 78
Egypt, 21, 58, 98, 144, 178
Eisek ben Yekel, 134-135
Elijah, 81, 91-92, 138-139, 144-145
Elohim, 68
Esau, 57
Eternal, 37
Ethics of the Fathers, 126
Europe, 101, 132, 168
Eve, 20, 78-79, 142

"Finders Keepers," 111
Five Senses, 42-43, 132
Forbidden Fruit, 78
Freedom, 58
Freedom of Will, 74, 76, 82
Fruit of the Tree (Forbidden Fruit), 79

Garden of Eden, 78
Germany, 54, 109
Golden Rule, 124
Good Whisper, 72, 74, 76
Greeks, 54, 105

Hadrian, 65
Hanukah, 174, 178
Ha-Shem (the Name), 68
Hassidic Song (Dudaleh), 132
Hassidim, 132
Hassidism, 136, 154, 156, 164-165
Heavenly Father, 68

189

Hebrew (language), 166-168
Hebrews, 55, 57, 157
High Priest, 68
Hillel, 88, 96, 105, 123, 175, 184-186
Hillel's Rule, 122-124, 126
Hitler, 54, 109, 144
Hiya bar Abba, 175
Holy Book, 167
Holy City, 179
Holy Land, 158
Holy Language, 167
Holy of Holies, 68
"House of Gathering," 160

"Image of God," 45, 51-52
India, 158, 162
Indians, 73
Isaac, 55, 157
Isaiah, 125
Ishmael, 57
Israel, 20, 93, 125, 167, 179
Israel, Children of, 80

Jacob, 55-56
Jerusalem, 58-59, 93, 123, 125, 158-163, 179
Joseph, 98-99
Joseph ben Levi, 144-145
Judea, 94, 124

Kaddish, 38, 168, 169
Kiddush, 58, 178
King Christian, 102
King David, 84, 108
Kingdom of God, 81
King of Denmark, 102
Kohanim, 158

Law (Torah), 21, 56-57, 186
Levites, 158
Levi Yitzhak, 154
Lot, 134

Maimonides, 93
Meir, 63
Mercy, 94-95, 97-99
Mezuzah, 68
Micah, 89, 106
Middle Ages, 93
Modim Anachnu, 180

Moon-god (woman god), 14
Moriah, Mount, 158
Moses, 21-22, 26, 56, 58, 63, 80, 85, 89, 107, 136, 158-159
Mount Moriah, 158
Mount Sinai, 89

Nathan, 84
Nazis, 54, 101-102

Palestine, 20, 158
Pappos ben Judah, 182
Passover, 58, 174, 178
Patriarchs, 56-57
Peretz, Isaac, 151
Phineas, 63
Pilgrims, 20
Poland, 109, 132
Polish, 109
Prague, 134
Prayer Book, 164-169
Prayer Shawls, 24
Priests, 159, 161-162
Private Prayers, 174-175
Promised Land, 157
Psalms, 158, 168
Purim, 178

Rav, 174
Reform Jews, 168
Repentance, 116-121
Rock (God), 68
Romans, 24, 54, 65, 94, 124, 182
Rome, 163
Russia, 132

Sabbath, 58, 69, 131, 151, 169, 170-171, 173-174, 180
Samaria, 92
Samaritan, 63
Seder, 174, 178
Self-Respect, 103, 122
Sephardic, 168
Services (Prayer), 161-162, 166
Service of the Heart, 155, 161
Set Prayers, 170
Set Services, 170
Shaddai, 68
Shalom, 125

Shalom Aleichem, 154
Shammai, 123
Shehecheyanu, 173
Sh'ma, 22, 58, 158, 168-169, 172, 186
Sh'moneh Esreh, 169
Siddur, 168, 173, 179
Simon ben Shetah, 112
Simon ben Yochai, 124
Sinai, Mount, 89
Slavery, 21, 58, 178
Sodom, 133-134
Solomon, 107-108, 110, 178
Story of Creation, 128
Sun-god (man god), 14

Talmud, 33, 50, 56, 65, 156, 185
Tarfon, 184
Tefillah, 152
Temple, 68, 93, 158-162, 182
Ten Commandments, 21, 28, 56, 88
Terach, 17, 19

Teshuvah, 120
Thinking Machines, 47
Torah, 21, 28, 33, 88-89, 123-124, 178, 182-186
Traditional Jew, 176
Tzedakah, 91, 94
Tzedek, 91

United States, 88, 93
Universe, 27, 29-30, 32, 35, 39-40, 42, 54, 56, 65, 80, 103-104, 178
Ur, 17, 20

World to Come, 77, 80, 128
World War, 109, 173

Yemen, 162, 167
Yetzer, 72
Yetzer Ha-ra, 72, 74, 77, 81, 86, 110, 114, 120, 123, 126
Yetzer Ha-tov, 72, 77, 82, 123, 126
Yom Kippur, 68, 120, 131-132, 176
Zusya, 136

191